Hello from Amish Country!

OUR FAMILY AND I all shout *hello* in your general direction!

"Marlin, what is *Plain Values* really about?"

Over the years, many people have asked me this question. I think it's because we share stories across such a wide spectrum of life. *Invited* is my answer. It is not only an anthology of our most impactful stories from our first 12 years of work, it captures the heartbeat of what we are about. As we have been invited into authentic community by our Creator himself, so we long to share life with friends, family, and total strangers on a deeper level, whatever that may look like.

On our cover is the McCauley home, where the first story you'll read takes place. Gabe, Mandy, and their family have walked through some incredibly tough things. When someone goes through the "deep end of the pool," it is a fight to hang on to joy while knowing this world will continue to break their heart. Life is truly full of paradoxes—"the first shall be last and the last shall be first"—you get the idea. We aim to dive headlong into those realities... without breaking anything.

To give you a better context of who we are and how we got here, allow me to share a bit more of our story. Lisa and I met in high school and our families became best friends. A few years later, we began dating and then married. After walking the infertility road, we both felt it was time to answer the calling on our hearts to adopt. It was during this time our prayers changed from asking the Lord to bring us children to, "Please bring us the children You want us to have and equip us to meet their needs." And He did.

We adopted all four of our children. Our oldest son is on the autism spectrum and was almost four years old when he was placed with us. He is now an adult and no longer lives at home. Our two in the middle both have Down syndrome, and our youngest son has Mosaic Down syndrome. We are so grateful for the way the Lord heard our prayers and filled our home with much joyful noise!

Inside these last twenty years and after a few moves, we have rooted ourselves deeply on our little homestead. Our chickens, sheep and goats, pigs, and Bassett hounds roam the hilltop with a lone guinea fowl, affectionately named Hovie Lister, begging anyone they see to toss them a treat. Our gardens and orchard continue to grow and keep our pantry filled. Lisa (a teacher by trade) has homeschooled our crew these many years. Sitting around a fire, working in the garden, cooking meals from scratch, and spending time together—these are the things we aim to be about.

So, fill a cup with something sweet or smooth, kick back, and let me personally invite you into the Plain Values family. Finally, next time you're in Winesburg, Ohio, please look us up and pop in. You can't miss the old stone house in the middle of town. Consider yourself *Invited*!

As always, may you find joy in the simple things. 🐦

Marlin Miller, Publisher
Always looking for more friends

WORDS BY:
Wendy Cunningham

Surviving the Unimaginable

"IT WAS APPARENT TO EVERYONE ELSE that we should be dating," Mandy McCauley says of her husband Gabe. Gabe, who was from West Virginia, met Mandy at a small, private Bible college in her home state of Florida. It wasn't immediately obvious to her, but their mutual friends were right: Mandy and Gabe were a perfect fit. Mandy aspired to be a singer/songwriter, and Gabe aspired to be with Mandy. The couple relocated to the Nashville area after college, where Mandy pursued her dream, and Gabe started a film production company.

After nearly a decade together, Mandy was in the process of putting out her first album when the couple was surprised to learn they were expecting a child. Because of her career choice, Mandy had resigned herself to start a family later in life—if at all—and felt this was coming at a bad time. "I was finally getting my shot." But she believed God was redirecting her towards something much bigger and more important.

The McCauleys could not have imagined the life change God had in store for them.

"There were some indicators before Scout was born that something was amiss," Gabe shares. The ultrasound revealed some abnormalities. "They could see that she had bilateral clubfoot, so that set off a series of protocols," Mandy adds. "We didn't really know what to expect or what that

would mean. But I prayed a lot." There was nothing the couple could do other than wait and see.

When Scout was born, she struggled to breathe and was immediately whisked away by the doctors. In addition to the clubfoot, the new parents were told their baby had a cleft palate, which was likely the cause of her breathing issues. But by day three, a cardiologist had discovered an abnormality in Scout's heart and she was transferred to Vanderbilt University Medical Center. That was the beginning.

Scout was born with a rare and relatively newly discovered connective tissue disorder called Loeys-Dietz syndrome. Although she was diagnosed early, which both parents say was a huge blessing, there were not a lot of answers to their growing list of questions. "We had very humble doctors," Mandy recalls. They just didn't know much because the condition was still so uncommon. They did know the life expectancy wasn't great—an average of 27 years—but there was a lot of hope in research at the time. The McCauleys held onto that hope because what else could they do?

At one month, Scout had her first heart surgery to repair holes. Her connective tissue would grow faster than other heart tissue, and so, at two years old, she underwent surgery to replace her aorta. She also struggled to eat well due to the cleft palate. She wore braces on her legs as they developed abnormally. Scout and her parents endured countless procedures and therapies as they navigated life with a child with special needs.

"Having Scout was the catalyst to a more genuine faith," Gabe confesses. "Having to deal with real life and real fear and hard questions—Why would God allow these types of things? Doubt is not the opposite of faith. It's just the other side of the coin." Gabe describes his faith journey as, "More erratic now. There is genuine joy and freedom, but also the depths and shadows are deeper."

Mandy also experienced a transformation in her faith walk as she stepped into her new challenging role of mom. "I always had a constant conversation going with God. I had faith that He knew better than me, and He was going to take care of us. From the moment the doctor said, 'Push,' we learned what was really important. Once that baby [was born], I realized, 'If I love this baby like this... God has to love me nine-thousand times more than I love this baby." Mandy's faith grew by leaps and bounds in those early months. Not only was she scared for and deeply in love with this new child, but she was also discovering new levels of love with her Heavenly Father.

"The Bible is not a law book. It's a love story," she adds. Becoming a mother was like an awakening for Mandy. "Having Scout made me fall more in love with God. How can you love someone if you don't have feelings for them? Before Scout, I didn't have 'feelings' for God." Mandy's faith went from being a noun—something that just existed as part of her life—to an experience. Scout ushered in an encounter.

Adding Scout to their family taught the McCauleys the beauty and importance of church community. Both Mandy and Gabe were brought up in a church that left the couple navigating some complexities in their faith walk. "Neither of us wanted Scout to ever wonder if she was going to heaven," Mandy says. Growing up, Gabe and Mandy struggled to fully grasp and appropriately apply concepts like forgiveness, shame, guilt, and

sin. There were shifts the McCauleys hoped to apply to the faith traditions they desired to pass onto their children. Having Scout brought about some of those shifts.

"I got to witness a Christian community support and encourage us in ways that I had not experienced before," Gabe says. "Having people who have special needs in society give the rest of us an opportunity to exercise community." Despite the immense challenges having a child with Scout's condition brings, the couple thought of it as a privilege to receive love and see the world through this new lens. It was still difficult, but it was also a gift. It brought purpose to their circumstances. When the McCauleys found out their close friends Rory and Joey Feek were expecting a baby with Down syndrome, Mandy said, "Congratulations!"

Gabe says, "We knew they were in for some of the most profound experiences."

When Scout was three years old, the couple welcomed another child—a boy. "[Ash was] in many ways what we needed," Gabe says. He brought a different kind of joy and light to their family dynamic. As Scout and Ash grew, they became best friends. Because Scout's condition is limited to her physicality, her mind is completely intact. Scout was thrilled to have a brother, a companion, and they loved each other deeply.

However, every child comes with a little added complication as well. The most difficult part about adding Ash to the mix was the complexity of having what is called an "unaffected child." Scout's condition demanded so much time and energy that it was hard for the couple to

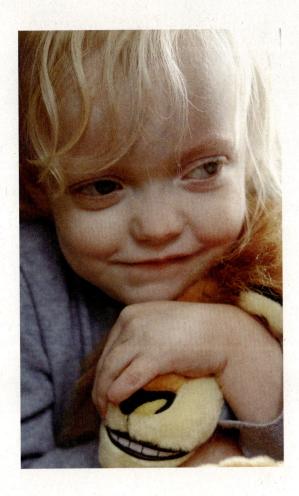

find the balance. There was a lot to contend with, and although there was a tremendous amount of joy in their growing family, there was also a lot of stress to navigate within themselves, their children, and their household.

Gabe and Mandy took a leap of faith and moved away from the Nashville area to Columbia, Tennessee. It was an act of faith because of how dependent they had become on hospitals and specialized medical care which was more readily available in Nashville. But the McCauleys desired a different way of life—a different pace. They needed a change. It was still difficult, but living on land away from the city offered a peace they had been longing for. And for a little while, their family fell into the rhythm of daily life.

Sadly, it was only for a little while.

One evening, Scout began complaining of pain. They took her to the hospital completely unaware that it would be her final trip. The next day, she was gone. On January 5th, 2019, Scout was fully healed and completely restored as she entered into eternity.

Gabe and Mandy were left to face the unimaginable.

It's not supposed to work this way. Parents aren't supposed to outlive their children. It's an unspoken agreement most of us believe we've entered into with God. And yet, the McCauleys' story reminds us that it does happen. Bad things do happen to good people. Tragedy strikes when we least expect it. And grief is never something anyone can see coming or prepare for.

Gabe borrows a phrase from a mentor when he says, "Progressive revelation. That's where I'm at with all of this." These things don't always make sense. They're hard to process. And although some days there is peace, it never really gets easier. But God is in it. He's showing them one step of the way at a time. "I've come to be comfortable sitting in the doubt and the darkness. I don't run from it."

"Scout was born in 2009. She lived nine years, nine months, and nine days…" Gabe recalls with tears in his eyes. "We have this thing with nines. Ever since our college years. We see nines everywhere." As he speaks, Gabe smiles and points across the coffee shop to a woman waiting in line. The back of her sweatshirt has a single number on it: nine. "One of my hopes is that we will redeem this someday. Maybe in nine years…"

What would redemption even look like? Purpose? Restoration? Peace?

Perhaps the McCauleys will know it when they see it.

"Scout has certainly shaped who we are," Gabe recounts. "First, special-needs parents and then parents who've lost a child." He pauses. "It would seem real growth only happens through suffering. I hate it."

Whether you're a parent or not, it's unimaginable to consider what this family has walked

through. Not just in Scout's passing, but in every step of the way until and since. Yet somehow, Mandy sums it up perfectly when she says, "This is the holy s**t." (Yes, she used a curse word because sometimes that's the only word that works.) Death is holy. Life is holy. They're also equally crappy. "The holy __ is the day-to-day stuff that you don't love but you know you have to do, and it's the right thing. It's the hard things. The things you do entirely out of love." These are the things Gabe and Mandy did day in and day out while Scout was with them. But it's also the things they've been doing ever since.

It's all a holy act. The act of living on this side of eternity.

Mandy adds, "This is the stuff of life—the holy ground of servitude and love that a lot of people choose to avoid." Mandy and Gabe certainly didn't choose any of this, but they recognize the sanctity

of every moment they shared with Scout. There is a whole lot of life in every one of those nine years, nine months, and nine days.

"We've experienced the sacredness and the brevity of life," Gabe summarizes.

There is remorse, but no regret.

When reflecting on what exists now in his life that wouldn't have been there if he'd not loved and lost Scout, Gabe says, "It has created an innate draw to develop and create community in small, unique, quiet ways." He smiles. "I imagine God has something to do with that."

Two years before Scout's passing, the couple's friend Rory Feek lost his wife Joey to cancer. Several men just showed up on Gabe's porch to sit with Rory in his grief. It was a gift. Much like that first week in the story of Job. "Porch Time," as it came to be called, allowed for a space to talk about the real stuff—things that really matter. And the people we become because of those things.

Two years later, the same group showed up to sit with Gabe.

"The Porch is a sacred place for slowing down. I used to think going slow was a detriment, but now I see it as a blessing."

Gabe now understands the importance of fostering and encouraging people to create this space for each other—not just in times of grief, but always. Because the transformative things of life are ongoing. But even though Gabe counts this space as a blessing, he struggles to articulate what "Porch Time" is. "When you try to define it, it starts to lose what it is. It's not something. It's nothing. That's the point. Just sit and be. No expectations. No conversation starters. There is no pitch, you don't have to talk at all actually. It's just a time for contemplation and reflection. But it's not approached flippantly either. It's creating intentional community."

Sometimes, in the busyness of life, we forget to slow down and connect. Grief has a way of making a way. "I don't know if I would have been able to do that, or prioritize community, if I hadn't gone through something really hard."

Mandy sees the blessings and lessons of having loved and lost Scout a little differently. Instead of what it brought into their lives, Mandy recognizes who they have become—or rather avoided becoming—and how they see the world differently because of knowing their daughter. "Scout saved our lives. I think we might have been jerks if she wasn't born. We could have been so much more selfish."

"Scout taught us that every single moment is precious and holy. You really don't know how much time you have," Mandy continued. "She was

a physical example of the precious gift of time and selflessness and joy in the midst of hard."

For Mandy, Scout was the embodiment of a living sacrifice: "I gave birth to what Christ is." In the same way Scout's birth brought about a newfound love for God, Scout's passing revealed a deeper understanding of why He sent Jesus. "There was nothing I wouldn't give to make it all better. I would have sacrificed my own life for that child."

The McCauleys get it. They're standing in the hardest, darkest, yet most illuminating place to see God's holiness.

Statistics vary, but some say the divorce rate of parents who have a child with special needs may be as high as 87%. Surprisingly, the statistics of divorce after parents lose a child are as low as 16%. No matter how you slice it, there is no question the McCauleys' marriage has weathered a tremendous amount of stress. The odds, it would seem, are stacked against them. And yet, somehow, they are stronger than ever. Their love and respect for one another is tangible.

"Gabe is my best friend. I just knew that I wanted to marry someone I really liked. A partner, not a lord," Mandy says. Part of their success lies in having picked the right person from the start. Although we never imagine we'll have to walk through tragedy like this with our spouse, standard wedding vows do promise "for better or for worse."

Gabe agrees that it does make a difference that their relationship was solid before any of this came to pass—they had been married for nine years before conceiving Scout. But he also concedes they are even closer now, on the other side.

> "We're allowed to hold deep sadness and immeasurable gratitude in the same memories. We can be broken and growing at the same time."

"We are stronger or better—although I don't like those words—because of the hard things. It's the hard things that have allowed us to hold onto each other even tighter." We're reminded of the refiner's fire and the purity that comes from going into the flames. "The idea of us not being a unit doesn't even ever cross my mind."

Mandy shares that it's complicated to navigate grief together, even when two people love each other well. There is no way around the ugly, you have to walk right through it. She confesses that for a while, they were in survival mode, fight or flight, doing what had to be done to survive. Perhaps they're still there some days. "If we're not honest, we will fall apart."

Gabe adds matter-of-factly, "We've been given the gift of bluntness and a lack of pleasantries." There is no room for facades or pretenses when you're surviving the unthinkable. It's all real. All the time. Mandy and Gabe have had to learn to communicate like never before. They have to ask each other for what they need. And more than anything else, they have to be vulnerable. But being vulnerable in grief can sometimes feel like a bottomless pit.

Mandy says she's learned to, "Be gentle. Read the room." She adds that they're in a constant conversation and always trying to stay on the same team. "It's not beautiful. It's messy."

"One of the harder parts has been parenting Ash through this," Gabe admits. "When kids deal with this type of grief, they have to deal with it at every stage of development as they grow." He tells about the cyclical nature of this process as Ash gets older. Each new leap in his mental and emotional development is met with fresh understanding of what has happened and

what's been lost. It's as if they lose Scout over and over again.

Mandy returns to the theme of "gentleness." With Gabe. With Ash. With herself. "Gentleness has been the instruction from God on how to navigate this whole process." Mandy is reminded of a phrase that's not her own but has brought her a lot of peace through the journey. "The Holy Spirit is a gentleman." She knows He's not going to force something on her that she's not ready for. He's patient. He's waiting. He's kind. And He never leaves. Despite God's goodness and ever-presence, Mandy admits she's still in the thick of it.

"I'm mad at God. I want it to go away, but it hasn't."

Her honesty brings clarity and peace to those who grieve along with her. This is hard. Impossible, really. And it's okay to not be okay. It's also okay to take steps forward. Neither forfeit what's important—neither hold much meaning. It's all just part of the process. We're allowed to hold deep sadness and immeasurable gratitude in the same

memories. We can be broken and growing at the same time. It's confusing. It's terrible. And it's wonderful.

What is most profound about the McCauleys' story is that their life was not changed when Scout died. Yes, that was a terribly challenging part of their journey, but it's not the catalyst for their transformation. The McCauleys' lives were changed when Scout was born. It's not her death that defines them, but her life. The mere fact that she was theirs, even for just a brief time, will forever outweigh the weeks and years they'll spend apart.

After all, time is short. Those weeks and years will be over soon enough. For all of us.

Scout is a gift. And her story is a blessing. It reminds us every day that we have a choice to make. We can allow life to bury us. We can let grief and pain be our whole story. Or we can choose to be marked by living—right in the midst of the mess. We can choose to cling tighter to God and to each other.

That's how we survive the unimaginable. 🐦

One Minute *with* Marlin

with **MARLIN MILLER**

Marlin Miller is the publisher of *Plain Values*. **He is an excellent storyteller, and we know you'll love his bite-sized messages.**

Storytime

Words by: Marlin Miller

Originally published in February, 2022

EVERY EVENING Adelaide, Bennett, and I have the same routine. After baths are done, teeth are brushed, and the many "night night love you's" are shared between the five of us, we begin. The doll babies are put to bed and tucked in their warm blankets. We find the tattered and coverless pictorial children's Bible, I read a story, we take turns saying a prayer, and then end our routine by taking turns singing "Jesus loves me." But in between, something wonderful happens. After I have read the story of the evening, Addie and Bennie compete for the Bible in order to "read a story to me!" And what "reading a story" consists of for them is scouring the Bible from front to back and finding the pages with photos of Jesus. Invariably, I am saying the words, "That's Abraham" or "That's not Jesus either, that is David. Jesus is in the back half of the Bible." In their Bible, Jesus is always wearing the same white and red clothes, and the squeals of delight when the kids find Him are unlike anything else.

When we are sitting together, I often wonder how much they comprehend what we are reading and talking about. They may never understand the human condition and how sin has destroyed much of what God originally created, but there is something inside our little boogers that draws them to Jesus. I think this is much more of a question being tossed into the air than a statement or an observation. I don't have an answer, but watching and hearing little children come to our Lord with a level of innocence and purity only those with Down syndrome can have is a blessing all its own. In Matthew 19:14, Jesus says, "Let the little children come to Me, and do not forbid them; for of such is the kingdom of heaven." Many times, I make life harder than it is. Maybe you can relate. I hope that tonight, when you and I sit with our families thinking and talking over the last day, we can search for Jesus hidden in the pages of our lives.

As always, may you find joy in the simple things. 🕊️

Porch Time

Words by: Marlin Miller

Originally published in June, 2022

ON A RECENT TRIP, we spent a few evenings with a wonderful family who lost a young child only a few years ago. We quickly became fast friends as we connected on a deep level, sharing the good and the hard as our kids ran and played. As we traveled home, I told Lisa there is a part of me that wants to skip all pleasantries in conversation from now on. She gently reminded me that not all folks are comfortable with jumping right into sharing deep, authentic thoughts, emotions, or parts of their lives. But this is what I long for—the kind of friendship built on solid foundations of hope only found in Jesus. My point is this... this life is so short, why do I want to spend time talking about weather that will change in ten minutes! A friend recently told me when he meets new folks and the conversation turns to work and occupation, he follows it up with this line... "Ok, you're an engineer, but what do you *really* do?" I love that because it digs underneath the surface and asks a deeper question to which most folks give a very different answer.

I am tweaking his question a little in certain circumstances... "Ok, but how are you *really* doing?" Everything we do here at Plain Values is centered around building and living in community. On that note, I feel I owe you an apology. For the last ten years, I have talked about living in community and loving our neighbors, but I haven't lived it out to its full capacity. So, beginning in June of this year, we are opening our office every third Friday of each month from 1pm to 4pm. I do not want to simply talk about living in community, I want to do it. I am sorry for the many conversations I should have shared with people I didn't make time for or did not catch the pause or pain in a short answer.

The same friend who buried his daughter a few years ago intentionally lives out his days at a slower pace. He makes time for his friends. I want to live in that pace as often as I can. A wise man told me regarding changes in life, "Often small is big. A small change lived out is bigger than a huge change that lasts for a week and is forgotten."

Every third Friday afternoon of each month, from 1:00—4:00pm EST, we're hosting Porch Time at Plain Values. During this time window, you're invited to come in, have a cup of coffee or tea, sit on the porch, and visit for a while. You might meet a few of our team and discover their role in building *Plain Values* each month.

As always, may you find joy in the simple things. 🐦

One Squirrely Christmas

Words by: Marlin Miller

Originally published in February, 2023

THE FAMILY IS SETTLING into the house that's going to be our home for the next three days. I've driven 500 miles, and I'm trying to catch a bit of rest on the couch before we head out to dinner with friends. Half awake, I hear a little scritching sound and little bits of creosote falling down the chimney, but I don't think much of it. Suddenly, a flash of fur hangs down from inside the fireplace, and I leap to my feet and jam the fire screen against the opening, all the while yelling, "Get outta here!" I cannot believe what a close call that was.

The next two days were even worse. Both of our moms and the three kids periodically had to stop what they were doing and run to the fireplace to chase the intruder back up the chimney. It was a game of cat and mouse, and our kids thoroughly enjoyed it! But then Saturday evening came. The event that we were going to was the purpose for the trip, and we all headed out the door soon after dinner. We discussed the fireplace situation, and I think I said something to the effect of, "Well, those things go to bed at night, don't they?" We came back to our home away from home, and as I walked in, I noticed a few Christmas decorations lying on their side by the fireplace, but again, I didn't think anything of it. As I walked on into the kitchen, I saw a wooden star lying on the kitchen floor next to a broken plastic plate. By this time, the rest of the family had made their way in and apparently realized what I had not, because I heard someone say, "Marlin, that squirrel is still in the house—it's got to be here somewhere!" We started looking under the couch and behind the furniture, and I checked the bedrooms. Not more than a few minutes later, someone hollered out, "It's in the Christmas tree!" And it was game on!

We got the kids downstairs, and I realized that we had a real problem on our hands. How in the world are we going to get this squirrel out of the house? We tried a few things, including trying to scoot the Christmas tree closer to the door, which only made the squirrel leap onto the curtains. At one point, my mom was trying to keep it at bay by the front door using two sweatshirts as weapons! After about fifteen minutes and much hollering, we had a squirrel locked in the bathroom. I will say, you have not lived till every single curtain has been violated, and you have squirrel scat on the kitchen floor! With the biggest trashcan I could find and a Styrofoam cooler lid, I marched into the bathroom to do battle—at least that's what it felt like! After a few minutes of high-pitched squealing (the squirrel's, not mine), I emerged victorious with the angry squirrel contained and wasted no time getting outside. What a wonderfully hilarious Christmas vacation memory!

If we only had an RV!

As always, may you find joy in the simple things.

Confessions *of a* Steward

with **JOEL SALATIN** | *Photos by:* **MILLPOND PHOTOGRAPHY**

Joel co-owns, with his family, Polyface Farm in Swoope, Virginia. When he's not on the road speaking, he's at home on the farm, keeping the callouses on his hands and dirt under his fingernails, mentoring young people, inspiring visitors, and promoting local, regenerative food and farming systems.

Beginnings

Words by: Joel Salatin

Originally published in September, 2021

DOES GOD CARE HOW I FARM? That question defines my life's work and vision because it moves the visceral, practical decisions I make in my farming vocation to a place of sacredness and godly living. If God cares about physical and practical things in my life, then my theology and belief structure are more than academic pursuits.

They are not just discussion groups and conversations. If God cares how I farm, then I should enthusiastically embrace searching for techniques and protocols that please Him. After all, it's all His stuff. The courthouse may say I own this land, but ultimately I don't. Legally and culturally I may advocate for property rights, but really it's all God's property. Does He care how it's handled? Does He care how I leave it? Does He care what I do with it?

By extension, does God care what my farm looks like on someone's plate? Does He care if my corn goes into factory-farmed chickens, high fructose corn syrup, or pastured pigs? Indeed, does what I believe in the pew show up on my menu? Does stinking up the neighborhood or polluting the water with lagoon run-off and chemical fertilizer adhere to the Golden Rule? If I owned North America, would I be pleased with a dead zone the size of Rhode Island in the Gulf of Mexico?

My dad's father wanted to be a farmer, but during the Depression he could not get a toehold. So he spent his life growing a massive garden and tinkering in his Indiana basement workshop. Post World War II, he became a charter subscriber to J.I. Rodale's *Organic Gardening and Farming Magazine*. That magazine launched the Rodale publishing house and extolled a biological approach to food production at a time when the chemical approach was not yet firmly embedded in our nation's psyche.

My dad wanted to farm but needed a nest egg. Already seeing the socialistic tendencies in the U.S. following World War II, where he flew in the Navy, he received a business degree on the GI bill, spent a year learning Spanish, then was hired on as a bilingual accountant for Texas Oil Company (later Texaco) serving the early oil development off of the coast of Venezuela. He saw South America as a new frontier, with plentiful cheap land and open markets. What better place to farm?

He married Mom (an Ohioan) and in just seven years saved enough to purchase a 1,000-acre highland Venezuela farm. Our family, which by 1957 included my older brother and me, moved to the farm and began raising chickens.

Joel and his parents during the early days of Polyface Farm

But alas, by 1959 political unrest enveloped the country, and our family became targets for the revolution that eventually unseated Peres Jimenez from power. Unable to procure protection, we fled and eventually returned to the U.S. on Easter Sunday 1961.

Dad left his heart and soul in Venezuela; he loved the culture, the people, the climate. Who wouldn't like a place where bananas, pineapples, and papayas grow wild? He hoped that once things settled down, we'd be able to go back; so rather than return to his midwestern roots, he looked at places within a day's drive of Washington D.C. in case the Venezuelan embassy called. Our family looked at properties from Lancaster, Pennsylvania, down through the Shenandoah Valley of Virginia, and as far south as Raleigh, North Carolina.

The embassy did not call. But we found a cheap place in Swoope, Virginia: a gullied rockpile that looked like the badlands rather than good land. Did I say it was cheap? We moved in during July 1961, and Dad immediately asked both public and private agricultural experts how to make a living on this 550-acre farm. All advisors agreed that we should graze the forest, plant corn, borrow more money, build silos, and buy chemical fertilizers.

My dad saw all this as a trap, a rat race, a chemical addiction. His dad (my grandfather) avidly promoted compost rather than chemicals. With three children to support (my sister was born late in 1961) and a mortgage to pay, he and Mom decided they couldn't make it without outside income. Mom taught high school health and physical education, and Dad was hired on as an accountant with a local firm.

On the side, he began experimenting on the farm, which was where his heart was. I'm now at the age where the older I get, the more I realize how smart and forward-thinking Dad really was. One of my most poignant childhood memories was a Sunday afternoon drive to visit a farmer who built mobile shelters. I can't remember what animal that farmer raised, but what I do remember is Dad's enthusiasm at the notion of mobile shelters.

Meanwhile, he began reading about rotational grazing. The terms mob grazing, high density grazing, or management intensive grazing had not yet been invented. Andre Voisin, author of Grass Productivity (still the iconic textbook in the grass farming movement), called it rational grazing (like rationing out the forage). In any case, Dad found this material early on and immediately began designing mobile electric fencing. Energizers were extremely primitive in those days.

By the mid-1960s, he had a functional system, and we began moving the cows every couple of weeks. We planted about 60 acres of gullied steep hillsides in pine trees to stop the erosion and get some ground cover. That reduced the open land from 160 acres down to about 90 acres, with the balance in Appalachian hardwoods with no access. My older brother wanted to raise rabbits, and

we built a mobile rabbit hutch with outlying runs like wings on an airplane.

After trying numerous ideas to keep the rabbits from digging out and escaping, we abandoned the pastured rabbit idea. Not wanting to discard something that could prove useful in a future iteration, we pulled those rabbit runs up in the rafters of the barn for safekeeping. A couple of years later, my fledgling laying hen enterprise (I got my first ones when I was 10) outgrew our little chicken coop behind the yard, and Dad suggested we pull those old rabbit runs down out of the rafters and put my chickens in them.

With a bit of retrofitting, they worked superbly and birthed pastured poultry on our farm. With both Dad and Mom working full time town jobs, our farm was an oversized homestead. We could only keep about 15 cows due to low fertility. When I began raking hay at about 13 years old, I would put 16 swaths together to make one anemic windrow. I could walk the whole farm and never set foot on a piece of vegetation; that's how much bare ground existed. Visitors would have thought we were raising thistles as a crop.

10-year-old Joel working on his chicken pens

We always milked a couple of cows by hand, churned our own butter, made our own yogurt and cottage cheese, and when I was about 13, began selling at the local curb market. It was a Depression-era farmers' market that enjoyed food safety exemptions if vendors were members of agricultural extension service programs. I joined 4-H to qualify, which enabled us to sell uninspected meat, milk products, cooked chicken, field-slaughtered and home-processed beef and pork. Every Saturday of the year from the time I was about 14 until I finished high school at 18, I got up at 4 a.m. to be down at the market by 6 a.m.

This period of time spanned 1970-1975; Vietnam; Woodstock; hippies. Looking back, I realize we were about a decade—or maybe two—ahead of our time. But we had loyal customers, gained invaluable marketing experience, and most of all realized the advantages of selling directly to retail customers. Wearing the processing, marketing, and distribution "middle-man" hats in addition to the production hat enabled even an extremely small farm to make a living.

The conversation that set the stage for the rest of my life occurred one morning with Dad out on the farm lane beyond the barn. One of his accounting clients was a realtor and, always on the quest for another property to list, queried Dad about selling. "You could sell this place for

"Does God care? Yes. And when we embrace His techniques, He fills our barns a hundredfold."

$500,000 and buy triple the acreage in Arkansas or Missouri," he said.

Dad, always the innovator and ready for the next big thing, did not dismiss the idea, and I got wind that he was pondering over it. I approached him on that farm lane one morning to confirm if I'd heard correctly. He asked me if I truly wanted the farm for my life's vocation (neither my sister nor brother were interested in farming), and I said I did. He promised to never consider selling again, and he never did.

From that moment on, my mind was consumed with how to make a living on this little farm. With only 90 acres of pasture and no access to the rest of it, how could I make a living? This was during the Nixon administration and the Watergate debacle. A junior in high school at the time, I worked Saturday nights at the local newspaper, writing police reports, obituaries, and other spot news items. I loved writing. As early as 9 years old, I would write fiction stories in spiral notebooks just for fun. We never had a TV (still don't), and this was part of my entertainment. I knew I had a flair for writing, speaking, and communication in general.

Why not become a journalist, write a bestseller, and then return to the farm with royalties? That seemed like a good path, so I headed to college since that's what smart kids are supposed to do, got an English degree, and returned to the

newspaper, living at home and working in town. Teresa and I married, fixed up the attic in the old farmhouse (we called it our penthouse), drove a $50 car, only ate what we grew in the garden, and saved every penny. Within a couple of years, we'd saved enough to live on for a year.

I resigned from the newspaper job and came home, assuming our little nest egg would run out in a year. But it never did. It was like the widow's cruse of oil; things were tight but we survived, direct marketing to local customers, starting back into broiler chickens, selling firewood, and living frugally. Today that has morphed into a $4 million farm business serving 6,000 families, 30 restaurants, numerous institutions, 20 paychecks, and four generations living on the farm.

The farm has responded to our care. Those 100-bale fields now yield 1,200. Those scant windrows are now too big to step over. Eroded soils have built up a foot over bare rocks. To watch God's abundance manifest itself in such a profound way brings us to our knees in gratitude. Does God care? Yes. And when we embrace His techniques, He fills our barns a hundredfold. As a result, the farm is now an object lesson of divine mercy and grace. We love showing visitors what He has wrought through our hands, heads, and humility. It's all God's stuff. 🐦

Vicarious Farming

Words by: Joel Salatin

Originally published in September, 2022

WHEN I WAX ELOQUENT about farming as a good and necessary vocation, even suggesting that we should have many more farmers (and fewer factory farmers), people often squirm and respond, "But all of us can't be farmers."

It's the same kind of response we often feel when sitting in a service emphasizing missions, and we find our inner heart saying, "But we all can't be missionaries." Or a sermon about helping the needy, and we respond, "But we all can't run a soup kitchen." You know the drill. If there's one thing worse than not being convicted when we're wrong, it's being incorrectly convicted when we're not wrong. Remember, Satan is the great Accuser. But in all these ministries, we can be vicarious participants, either directly or indirectly, through prayer, offerings, and an attitude of helpfulness.

We need plumbers, electricians, welders, sawmill operators—you know the list. Farming tends to be vocationally higher on my list because it's the front line of creation stewardship. Farming shapes God's landscape—air, soil, water, trees—more dramatically and directly than any other human activity. Indeed, Rev. 11:18 says God will "destroy those who destroy the earth." Stewardship is near and dear to God's heart.

"No occupation is so delightful to me as the culture of the earth"

Thomas Jefferson

Just like all of us should have a heart that leans into missions or helping the needy, we should have a heart that inclines toward farming because creation care is something God mentions specifically. So how do those of us who aren't farmers participate, or at least incline responsibility, just like we do with missions or philanthropy?

The first attitude is to care. That's not as trite as it sounds. Interest precedes activity. Intention precedes movement. As we cultivate care toward farming, the obvious first question is what kind of farming God wants. Does God care about farming modality? Are all farmers doing good, or are some doing bad? Just like we would vet a missions program, adoption program, or any other philanthropic endeavor, we must vet farming.

An exercise I like to encourage folks to cultivate is when you sit down to eat, look through your plate to the other side, and envision the kind of farming that puts those morsels on the plate. If you need to squint your eyes, that's fine. Ha! Look at the food and imagine everything behind it.

Provenance includes numerous threads. The farmer as producer is one, but it also includes the processor, the distribution network, marketing, and point of sale. As you squint through your plate to the other side, ask some salient questions:

- Does this food **build soil** or destroy it?
- Does this food **honor the workers** who brought it to my table?
- Does this food **maximize nutrition** or minimize nutrition?
- Does this food **respect and honor the beings**—both plant and animal—that sacrificed for my sustenance?
- Does this food **encourage understanding** or ignorance about how it was grown, handled, and brought to my plate?

- Does this food make **neighbors happy** or unhappy—smells and appearances?
- Does this food **help my community** emotionally, economically, and environmentally or jeopardize those elements?
- Does this food **engender transparency** or opaqueness?
- Does this food **honor biology** or mechanics?
- Does this food bring rural and urban populations **closer as friends** or does it alienate and segregate?

As we take each item on our plate and run it through this battery of questions, we can see where it falls on a continuum of sacredness. Perhaps the most important question to any of these queries is: "Does God care?" Does God care if farming techniques erode the soil? Does God care if we create a dead zone the size of Rhode Island in the Gulf of Mexico? Does God care if we stink up the neighborhood?

We could ask the same questions about any of our more ministry-oriented activities. Does God care how missions are done? How the gospel is preached? What organizations receive our offerings? I've found that the faith community loves discussing these issues, but suddenly when it comes to food and whether Chick-fil-A is what should be on our plate, we clam up and look the other way.

Just like we are admonished to take on the sufferings of Christ, the sufferings of persecuted Christians, and the needs of widows and orphans as a means of identification and interest, we can take on farming by identifying as fellow participants with the food we choose to put on our plates. Is the landscape created by our food dollars the kind of landscape we want for our children? Is it one that honors God's creation?

These simple questions are profound because they force us to wrestle with difficult issues. But beyond that, they bring us to a place of interest, as partners, in farming as a land-healing ministry or a land-debilitating exploitation. The earth is certainly a jewel of God's creative power; If we eat, we impact how it's handled. Whether we farm for a vocation or farm vicariously, through our food choices, we are all farmers. Identifying intentionally with our food origins, processing, and distribution is the first element in vicarious farming.

A second element is developing a relationship with farmers. Just this morning, my wife Teresa and I spent about an hour-and-a-half at a nearby U-pick fruit farm picking a couple gallons of unbelievably succulent non-chemical blueberries. Although we farm full time, we don't grow everything we eat. We could probably survive on only what we grow, but life is much richer when we develop mutually interdependent relationships. Few are as enjoyable as food relationships.

We helped this young farm couple stay in business, spoke encouraging words to them, and learned a little more about blueberries. In like manner, for years, we've gone to a nearby apple orchard and purchased a dozen bushels of apples to make our own applesauce. It's the best applesauce in the world, and this farmer knows we happily take seconds. We get a price break, and he has somewhere to go with his off-perfect product. We always ask how we can help with a problem item. That's the way to help a farmer's infirmities, so to speak.

Be the patron looking to solve the farmers' problems. Cracked eggs? Apples with some rust? Crooked green beans? Chicken necks and backs? Every farmer has slow movers; by shouldering that burden, you endear yourself to the farmer and step into his shoes of need. While certainly farming has its romantic and joyful moments, it's more often a bit lonely and definitely a slog. By appreciating imperfections and difficulties, you come alongside the farmer as a best friend; you may never know how you ministered to the farmer with that kind of strategic patronage or the encouraging word.

The closer you can get physically and emotionally with your farmer, the more you can be a vicarious farm participant. When your tomatoes come from a thousand miles away through a nameless, faceless chain of industrial processors, warehouses, and cash registers, you can hardly vet the God-honoring provenance of the tomato. Shorter chains of custody encourage authenticity in your food choices.

Over the years, we've had customers stuff money in our pocket after a particularly trying drought. One sold us a car for $1. Another offered us interest-free money in order to expand our cow herd at a strategic juncture. You might be amazed at the number of ways you can come alongside a farmer if you know the needs. You don't get that opportunity at Wal-Mart. Vicarious farming and relationships go together like a hand in a glove.

Finally, vicarious farming includes growing something yourself. It may be as simple as a quart jar of mung bean sprouts on the windowsill. It could be a vermicomposting kit under the kitchen sink. Lots of urban-gardening infrastructure is available, like hanging PVC pipes with pockets on the side to grow your own fresh herbs on the porch. These take up no more room than a big set of wind chimes, but they put your hands and head directly into the majesty and mystery of growing something.

In my book *Polyface Micro*, I detail how to have chickens and rabbits in an urban apartment—without noxious odors. Of all the farm animals, laying chickens are probably the most valuable and certainly the most doable on a tiny scale. Incorporating growing something into your life will put you in touch with living but also dying. As a highly developed culture, Americans today live in a highly sanitized, segregated context. For many, the only non-human life interaction is with a pet cat or dog. While that is nice, it

can often create a jaundiced view about the role of animals in the world.

Last year I debated animal welfare guru Peter Singer on the topic: "Animals should not be on our plate." These kinds of discussions are not indicative of a newly-evolved spiritual consciousness, but are rather indicative of a profound devolution resulting from disconnection to farming and food production. A sanitized and sterilized existence leads to all sorts of folly, and the "my cat is my aunt is my dog is my child is my chicken" mentality is only one of many.

Participating in the life and death cycle, viscerally and practically, add reason and humility to the human experience. While growing some herbs or a couple of chickens may not qualify you as a bona-fide farmer, it does bring you into a farmer's frame of reference. When your oregano plant dies, you step into the farmer's life. When the seed sprouts, you soar to the farmer's joy. These extremes help you appreciate the highs and lows of farming.

I'm certainly glad not everyone is a farmer. Who would buy my stuff? But I do love our patrons who make themselves one with us, identifying with both needs and opportunities. Anyone can join the farm team. When you eat, what kind of farm team are you building? We can all be vicarious farmers.

Fake Meat

Words by: Joel Salatin
Originally published in March, 2023

THE CURRENT DARLING of the industrial food system is fake meat or lab meat. Proponents argue that this will save the planet from the ravages of domestic livestock, offer better nutrition, and eliminate the ethical and moral dilemma of killing things for human sustenance. I'll deal with the first two quickly to put attention on the third one, which can be a stumbling block for people of faith.

The "animals are destroying the environment" mantra has numerous flaws, but the biggest one is that 500 years ago, the world had more pounds of animals on it than it does today, including people. In other words, if you could put all terrestrial non-plant life on a scale, the weight centuries ago is more than it is today. In fact, in the U.S., the pounds of domestic livestock have not changed in more than a century. In 1900, a third of the weight was in draft power: mules, horses, and oxen. Even with industrial factory farming, the total pounds of animals has not exceeded what it was in 1900. I'm including wildlife here as well.

Clearly animals are not the problem. I agree that the protocols to raise animals in confinement are not ecologically beneficial but blaming animals for farmers' failure is neither honest nor fair. Animals can be—and have been—grown in ecologically beneficial ways for millennia. The deepest soils on the planet are all under grasslands, not forestlands.

The second argument is about nutrition. Supposedly red meat increases the risk of cardiovascular problems and colon cancer. The only problem with this notion is that America's per capita consumption of beef has been falling annually for the last thirty years, while these diseases have been increasing. Without getting into the scientific nitty-gritty, the *red meat = disease* theory simply doesn't stand the test of even cursory perusal.

But what about this moral and ethical dilemma? It's touted by fake meat proponents in every flier, every news interview. It's a big deal. As a livestock farmer, I've certainly been accused of being a murderer or being unable to love because I kill animals. This sentiment is not going away; in fact, it's getting stronger by the day. As a Christian, I really don't like to be called a murderer.

> ## "As a livestock farmer, I've certainly been accused of being a murderer or being unable to love because I kill animals. This sentiment is not going away..."

A bit of historical context can help us appreciate the roots of this issue. The year 1837 was an interesting confluence of three things. First, a British scientist named Charles Darwin set sail on The Beagle. Father of evolution, Darwin's observations led him to conclude the biblical creation narrative is a myth and that humans evolved from monkeys. He took God out of life.

The same year, an Austrian chemist named Justus von Liebig, trying to solve the soil fertility problem, used vacuum tubes to isolate nitrogen, potassium, and phosphorus (NPK), announcing to the world that all of life is simply a rearrangement of these three elements. Think about how that supplemented Darwin's ideas that God wasn't necessary. Life was simply an inanimate pile of protoplasmic structures.

The third 1837 occurrence was Cyrus McCormick's invention of the reaper in his blacksmith shop on the family farm in Raphine, Virginia. This is now viewed as the official start of the Industrial Revolution because it made the scythe obsolete. McCormick's reciprocating cutter bar is still the backbone of modern grain and forage harvesting equipment. With Darwin's Godless existence, Liebig's lifeless existence, and McCormick's mechanical invention, the new enemy of biblical faith was not paganism, animism, or pantheism; it was no-theism and a mechanical view of life.

Gradually, life became less about biology and more about mechanics, physics, and chemistry. Today's effort to take life out of food is a natural extension of taking biology out of life. We should not be surprised that artificial food follows artificial fertilizer. Our nation has embraced artificial food for some time, from squirtable cheese to high fructose corn syrup.

The foundational idea that you can have life without death is not only fairly new in human history but is also fundamentally an assault on truth. Something has to die in order for something else to live. Everything is eating and being eaten. Lie down naked in your flower bed for a week and see if that's not true. Or in the pig pen.

Nothing provides a more poignant object lesson of Jesus's sacrificial gift of life than when an animal gives its life for human sustenance. The problem is that our western culture does not ascribe spiritual and attitudinal protocols to our domestic livestock. The average person does not see farmers asking how to make happy pigs or how to respect the pigness of pigs, in normal agriculture.

What the average person sees are agricultural experts seeking only four objectives: how to grow pigs fatter, faster, bigger, and cheaper. They aren't asking how to make pigs happy. They view pigs as mobile piles of inanimate protein to be manipulated however cleverly human imagination can conceive. For folks who do think it matters how we treat pigs, such thinking is egocentric, selfish arrogance in its worst manifestation.

Too many Christians make fun of these folks who care, rather than repenting of our own disrespect and mindless exploitation of the beings God entrusted to our management. It's not just nuts and bolts in a bucket; these are beings, much lower than humans, to be sure, but beings that need our stewardship nonetheless. No less than bumblebees and earthworms.

The other issue that clouds thinking today is the ubiquitous disconnection from life and death. For the average person, pets represent the only

animals in their personal frame of reference. When the only animal you ever encounter has a name and sleeps in your bed, it fosters a jaundiced view of animals in general. Suddenly every cow is a dog. Every chicken is a cat. Every pig is a pet gerbil. I've actually debated with people who said since I had no problem killing a chicken, I'd probably have no problem coming to their house and killing their cat.

Interestingly, we then have both the desecration of life on the one hand and the inordinate elevation of it on the other. Combine that with a disconnection to the barnyard, and you have a recipe for dysfunctional philosophy.

Sacrifice can be either sacred or sacrilege, depending on the circumstances. For example, the thieves crucified with Jesus on the cross do not elicit our sympathy; they were bad guys being punished. Nothing is sacred about their sacrifice. Jesus' sacrifice is sacred because He didn't do anything to deserve it.

In like manner, nothing is sacred about the sacrifice of an industrial factory-farmed chicken; it was never respected as a chicken in its life. Dispatching that chicken carries no emotional impact. But a chicken you raised, fed, watered, protected, loved—that sacrifice occupies sacredness in our thinking. It's how we honored and respected the being in life that makes the sacrifice sacred or sacrilege.

> "Eliminating death from life does not indicate some new elevated plane of spiritual nirvana; it's a devolution into profound misunderstanding about what true life, what true living, depends on."

When the proponents of fake meat invoke the moral and ethical dilemma argument, of course, they do not separate the two kinds of sacrifice as I've just done. It's not that nuanced for them. What they do know is that animals in western domestic livestock culture are not respected; they're not in a habitat that engenders happiness. With one broad swoop of fake meat, therefore, they think we can rid the planet of this kind of atrocity.

The problem is that you can't have life without death. A compost pile is a shining example of the life, death, decomposition, and regeneration cycle. Indeed, the regenerated compost, ready to feed new life, looks nothing like the components that went into the pile initially. The finished compost doesn't look the same, smell the same, or feel the same. I love reaching down and picking up handfuls of compost; manure, not so much. Manure after composting is wonderful; you can put milk on it in a bowl and eat it for breakfast. That's a joke. But it's really good-smelling stuff.

How do I truly live? I lay down my life for others. This is fundamental to biblical living, but the faith community too often fails to apply the respect for the sacrifice prior to death in order to make it a sacred thing. The sacrificial lambs of the pre-Christ Israelite object lesson were chosen carefully, often raised as pets. This connection brought to each person the specialness of life and the gift of death.

Eliminating death from life does not indicate some new elevated plane of spiritual nirvana; it's a devolution into profound misunderstanding about what true life, what true living, depends on. When Liebig dismissed earthworms, actinomycetes, and the billions of soil microorganisms as critical for life, he missed an important truth. In fact, he was incredibly wrong, and the world is still suffering from the simple NPK mentality he brought forward with such assurance.

Sometime in the future, fake meat will be found to be as lacking to sustain life as NPK to sustain fertility. Sometimes it takes a while for the truth to come out, but it does eventually. When someone exalts their spirituality by claiming nothing has to die in order for them to eat, you can ask them, "Why are you opposed to sacrifice?" See where the conversation takes you.

Indeed, our intestines are full of beings eating each other. Everywhere we look, we see life and death. On our skin. In our immune systems. The notion that we can have life without death is not only wrongheaded, it's antithetical to the gospel's core message. Food and farming offer wonderful object lessons to represent truth to our world; let's be consistent in the physical aspects of the object lesson so we can be attractive in the spiritual aspects. 🐦

Roots
+
Wings

with RORY FEEK

Rory Feek is a world-class storyteller, songwriter, filmmaker, and New York Times best-selling author. As a musical artist, Rory is one-half of the Grammy-award-winning duo, Joey+Rory. He and his wife Joey toured the world and sold nearly a million records before her untimely passing in March 2016.

to the
woods

"I went to the woods because I wished to live deliberately, to front only the essential facts of life, and see if I could not learn what it had to teach, and not, when I came to die, discover that I had not lived."

— Henry David Thoreau

Words by: Rory Feek
Originally published in October, 2022

NOW THAT WE'VE RETURNED home from being out West and are back at the farm here in Tennessee, I've decided to take some time off... a year off, to be exact. Not a year off work, but off the internet.

It may seem strange to write a column about taking a year off the web for a magazine where most of its readers are Amish who don't often use the internet anyway. The desire to unplug—or, more honestly, to understand why it could be important to do so—is already there for Plain people. But for me and the journey I'm on, these are new things that I'm still discovering.

I've been thinking about disconnecting for a good while now, thinking seriously for the last year or so. If you've read some of my earlier columns, you know that I've been slowly 'dumbing-down' my phone and simplifying our vehicles and lives to be more present in my life and community. Last summer, I took a hiatus from the web for a month and, since then, felt called to go deeper. Up until now, I hadn't found the right time to make the choice and commit to it. And so, as Indy and I were pulling away from the lodge in Montana, I took one last look at Google maps on my laptop, wrote down directions for the 1,750-mile drive home, disabled wi-fi, and off we went "to the woods."

My hope is that by disconnecting from the web, I can connect on a deeper level here at home with our farm, land, and community—with my family and friends, with God, and with the things that truly matter in life. I'm 57 years old, and who knows how much time I, or any of us, have. I want to live deliberately.

I love the Thoreau quote about his time at Walden Pond and his desire "to front the essential facts of life, and see if I could not learn what it had to teach, and not, when I came to die, discover that I had not lived." For me, here at our farm a half-century later, my journey "to the woods" is less about the actual woods and more about going to a place we don't know, where most other people aren't, to see what I can learn there. To see what it has to teach me about life so that I don't look back and say "I wish I had..." or wonder "what if."

Most of my family and friends think I might be a little crazy. They mostly love their smartphones and iPads and all the things the web brings to their lives. For them, the ease of having access to everyone and everything all the time is wonderful. They love that they can push a button and Amazon will deliver whatever their hearts desire to their doorstep the next day.

For me, it's more complicated than that. I'm not sure I want those things all the time. As a matter of fact, I'm sure I don't want them all the time. I want something more than just more stuff. Or more information. Honestly, I want less of most of these things.

After you've had GPS on your smartphone or vehicle for the last ten years or so, it can be a bit of a shock to your system to hold a Rand-McNally map in your lap again and try to make your way through downtown St. Louis, looking for the sign that will get you onto I-64 South. But after a day or two of doing it, and a few missed exits, I began to actually enjoy not knowing what was ahead of me. It's a bit of a lost art; driving with a map, or even more so, remembering directions in your head and reading road signs. Like everything else, we utilize these devices so that we can be freed up to do more important things when we drive like... well, I'm not sure

Packing the van for the ride back home to Tennessee

what's more important than that, but still most everyone chooses their destination and lets their phone or car tell them how to get where they're going these days.

My smartphone or car doesn't know how to get where I'm wanting to go. I'm headed to a place back in time, to a decade or two ago when these things didn't exist. To a time when we still had our problems, but they weren't digitally compounded in the way that they are today. I just want to unplug from the great big world and plug into the little one I'm part of.

After three days of driving, we got home here to Tennessee safe and sound. After unpacking, the first thing I did was unplug the internet router at the farmhouse. And just to be sure it was off, I climbed up onto the roof of the back porch and cut the United Internet cable that was running to the house.

There was something liberating about cutting that cord. Something that made it feel like I was doing much more than just turning one cable into two with wire-cutters. I was embarking on a new journey. And although the decision was mine, I wasn't going on this adventure alone. In cutting that cable, I knew I was taking Indy with me on this journey too. Gone for the next year are the Disney movies she loves to watch, the endless music we could listen to on Spotify, and the ability to FaceTime far-away family and friends on the computer. These things will be replaced by a silence that is already taking a bit of getting used to, but I know in time it is going to be so good for us.

I also knew, in another way, we were taking our family and coworkers on this journey with us as well. They all know that things are changing and that to come over to dinner, we've asked them to make sure their TVs are off. And since most of my work for the last ten years or so has been connected to the internet in one way or another, that too is going to be a big challenge for them, for all of us.

And although I'm not really sure how it's all going to work out yet, I believe that it's going to somehow turn out to be the best thing for us. The closing of that door for the next year will open another one that wasn't available before.

Last night, when dinner was through and bath-time was over, it was just Indiana and me here at the farmhouse. And it felt so good. It's been just us for the last six years, but strangely, when a house, even this old farmhouse, is hooked to the internet, it doesn't really feel like you're alone. It still feels like you're connected to everyone and everything.

As I held her in my arms and she read to me before bed, I realized how thankful I am for this time. Thankful that I can take this time to go "to the woods," to be truly, truly with her. Now. When she's eight years old and not look back someday and wish that I had. 🐦

cancel culture

"You can hardly go a week without hearing in the news about someone who has been caught in a lie or some facts about his or her past have been revealed, and they've been 'canceled'..."

— *Rory Feek.*

Words by: Rory Feek

Originally published in May, 2023

IN THE LAST DECADE OR SO, there's been story after story of celebrities and influential people, along with regular everyday folks, who have been "canceled." You can hardly go a week without hearing in the news about someone who, no matter what their life was before—what good they may have done in the long or short life they've lived so far—has been caught in a lie, or some facts about his or her past have been revealed, and all that they've done or been is suddenly null and void... replaced, it seems, by an unforgivable sin or story that now becomes the sum total of their life.

I've watched this happen again and again and seen the damage it does, not only to the people who have often made a mistake or struggled with something that they couldn't get a grip on—but also to people who may not have done anything wrong at all, or the facts haven't been checked before the story is spread. Either way, they are judged guilty by the media, mostly by a rapid viral-spreading on social media, until proven innocent. And, if and when that happens, and they've made reparations, or the truth has been revealed, the news has often moved on to the next attention-grabbing headline, and the real story never gets through.

I can't help but wonder what if, instead of being a "cancel culture," where we're so quick to condemn and forget any good thing anyone has ever done, we were a "redemption culture," where our first thought was of their pain, of their struggle, and were quick to forgive and believe in the hope of their tomorrow.

What would happen if the most virally spread news stories, the things that caught and kept our attention, were stories of people who have made mistakes in the past and are working hard to become new? If our concentration was on the good that people are doing, in spite of the missteps or bad choices they've made

in the past. What if our focus was on tagging someone *redeemed* and *worthy* rather than canceled and unworthy?

I'm not saying there aren't some horrendous things that have been discovered about people or that damage hasn't been done that should be accounted for. I just think as a culture, especially for us as Christians, we should remember that Jesus was all about repentance and redemption. It's why He came and why He died. To take away the stains of our sin and make our hearts pure and white as the snow. When I became a Christian, every single mistake, bad choice, or wrong turn I ever made was forgiven in an instant. I was no longer defined by what I did, or who I was, but instead by who I am now, and who He's going to make me into in the future. Ironically, God's message is exactly the opposite of the message our cancel-culture sends.

"I have always loved the word *redemption* and the power that it has in all our lives. It reminds me that it doesn't matter what our yesterday was... our tomorrow can be different."

Another concern, especially in this digital age where information and misinformation spread like wildfire with the push of a smartphone button, is that it creates fear in all of us. Fear that we won't live up. That we'll make some mistake, big or small, and be found out and humiliated and ultimately canceled. Unfollowed. Deleted. And that is a tragedy.

First off, it's incredibly sad that so many of our young people seem to find so much of their personal validation in the number of followers they have on Instagram, or how many views a photo or video they've shared has received, but also that they now have to live in fear of something that, honestly, most of the time isn't even real. I've been taking a sabbatical from the web for nearly a year now, and if somewhere during that time I was canceled, I'm not sure I would even know about it. I'm sure my friends or family would let me know and be worried for me, but since my day-to-day life—my *real* life—isn't about clicks or metrics or followers, I doubt it would change much.

Because I have a considerable online presence and am human, I completely expect to be canceled sooner or later. I don't think it's possible to be someone who has a positive story and following to not fall from digital grace at one time or another. It's bound to happen. Whether what they say or report is true or not, it doesn't really matter online. But in the actual world, it does. And luckily, I've been forgiven for my shortcomings, and I will be forgiven again. When I make mistakes in the future—and I will—I hope I'm quick to apologize and repent and start over with a clean slate. And though I know God will forgive me, I hope those around me, who know me and love me, will also forgive me and stand beside me as I begin again, new and redeemed.

And when those around me fall, as I know they will, I want to be the kind of friend who'll stand beside them, a friend who'll brush them off and walk with them 'til they get their footing again. I don't want to be someone who'll judge them, turn away, and leave them in their greatest time of need.

I have always loved the word *redemption* and the power that it has in all our lives. It reminds me that it doesn't matter what our yesterday was... our tomorrow can be different. Each and every day, we have the opportunity to turn from our mistakes and walk a new, better path. And I'm always watching for stories of redemption, whether in movies like Hoosiers, where coach Norman Dale overcomes his stormy past, or my nephew Mikel who, after years of struggling with alcohol, gets sober and begins building

a life he never dreamed was possible. But both of those, and all redemption stories, have to have a moment where a person hits absolute rock bottom. And it's only there, at that moment, that they can rise from the ashes to become what they were always born to be.

The truth is, when I hear a story about a celebrity or someone who has fallen from grace online, someone that the world has canceled, my heart breaks for them. My first thought is of the opportunity and blessing in this low moment because I know what an incredible story can follow it.

The next time you hear a story about someone being canceled, try to remember that we are all human, and we're bound to fall short while we're here on earth. Chances are they are like you and me, and they've done some good things in their lifetime, maybe even some incredible things, but we are all going to make mistakes. This is the moment when their humanity can be turned into hope. The question isn't if they have—or we have—walked a sin-free path. What really matters is how quickly we get back on track when we wander off.

Let's not be quick to cancel. Instead, let us be quick to forgive. For this is how redemption stories are born. 🐦

speak love

> "We need to speak into our kids.
> Because if we don't, the world will…"
>
> — *Rory Feek*

Words by: Rory Feek
Originally published in October, 2023

EVERY NIGHT AT BEDTIME, when I tuck our little girl Indiana in, I sit beside her and hold her hands, look into her little almond eyes and say, "Indiana, God made you very special, for a special purpose, and someday if you trust Him and you follow Him, He will show you." Indy always smiles great big and says, "Yes Papa, He will." And I know she believes it.

Little Indiana is special. Special to me. And also, I believe, to God. Not because she has Down syndrome—although she does have only one line across the palm of her hand, and an extra 21st chromosome. She's special to me because her Mama passed away when she was only two—through and in Indy, her mother lives on in our lives. And one day, when my time on earth is through, she and her sisters will be what is left of me. But Indiana is also special because God made her unique. One of a kind. The only one of her that has ever been or ever will be. He made her exactly who she is, on purpose, for a purpose. And I want to make sure she knows that. And speaking that into her, over her, is powerful. I know it is.

I also have two older daughters, Heidi and Hopie who are in their mid-thirties, and I so wish I could go back in time and speak into them as little ones, the way I do with Indy now. But I was young when I had them, and it would be a long time before I would have any idea there was even such a thing as purposefully speaking life and love into a child.

A few years ago, I was invited to a friend's house, along with about a dozen other men, for his son Sam who was turning 13. Men gathered around Sam, speaking into and praying over him. We sat in the living room of their house, and one by one we shared words of wisdom with this boy, who was becoming a young man. Sam

who go there with Indiana. Indy has Down syndrome, one of the little boys has an arm that doesn't work, and another has a heart condition that requires him to wear a monitor. But most of them are typical and wouldn't technically be labeled as special needs. The truth is, they all—we all—have special needs. Unique things that each of us need to grow to be the best person we can be.

At our school, and most school's, it's easy to get caught up with our kids, worrying about what we're teaching or not teaching them. Are they learning to read fast enough, memorizing their timetables, learning what other kids are learning, etc... But I try to remember that we are not really raising kids. What we're raising at our school, and in each of our homes, are adults. One day, in the not-too-distant future, they will be grown. Like you and me. People trying to figure out why they're here. What their purpose is and what really matters in life. So, more than anything, we need to speak life and love into our kids.

Besides speaking love into our children, I also believe that we desperately need to speak it into each other.

After that day when men gathered around and spoke into my friend's son, I went home thinking about it, and how at 50-something, no one had ever spoken into me. Some friends and I began talking about it, and on my next birthday, six or seven of my friends gathered around and

just sat quietly, respectfully listening to each one of us, taking it all in and saying "thank you" after each of us were through. It was easy to see how much it meant to him, and how good it was for him to hear these things, especially at such a critical age in his young life.

Now, that might not seem like a big deal to you, but for me—and the trailer parks I was raised in—it was as foreign as meeting someone from the moon. So, after that day, I began speaking into and over Indiana, and I try to do it every night. I can see the importance of directly affirming them and believe that we desperately need to speak into our children, and grandchildren, telling them how special they are, and that God has a purpose for their lives.

Because the fact is, if we do not speak love into our kids, the world will. But it speaks something else. It mostly says, "You aren't good enough, smart enough, pretty enough." They grow up feeling like they're too dumb, too fat, too old, or too poor for God to do something incredible with their lives.

We have a one-room schoolhouse at our farm with a full-time teacher and a dozen children

---

> **"I try to remember that we are not really raising kids. What we're raising at our school, and in each of our homes, are adults. So, more than anything, we need to speak life and love into our kids."**

---

spoke into me. One by one, they affirmed and encouraged me. And they prayed over a fifty-something-year-old like he was a thirteen-year-old just coming of age. Because in many ways, as strange as it sounds, I *am* just coming of age—just now beginning to understand the purpose God has me here for. And I can't begin to tell you how much their words, their time, and their love mean to me.

Since then, we have begun gathering around and speaking into other men in our group, no matter how old they are. Mostly because in our world today, no one has ever spoken into them, shared with them how special and loved they are. All around me each day (although I'm not doing as well at it as I'd like), I try to speak goodness and hope into friends and family. Because, again, we all know, the world is not.

Often, we speak into people just by being with them. By standing beside them in difficult times. By helping them when they need it most but are too proud to ask. Who knows what a difference it might make in someone's heart if we only try. It reminds me of a phrase that I heard years ago...

"Speak love...

and if you have to, use words." 🐦

HOMESTEAD SCHOOL
AT HARDISON MILL

The Healing Land

with **SHAWN & BETH DOUGHERTY**

Shawn and Beth Dougherty live in eastern Ohio, where their home farm is 17-acres designated by the state as "not suitable for agriculture." Using grass as the primary source of energy, they raise dairy and beef cows, sheep, farm-fed hogs, and a variety of poultry, producing most of their food, and feed, on the farm. They are also the authors of *The Independent Farmstead*.

Photo by Landon Troyer Photography
Edits by Seth Yoder

THE WAY HOME

Words by: Shawn & Beth Dougherty

Originally published in January, 2023

FROM WHERE OUR HOUSE IS PERCHED, halfway up the south slope of Wallace Hill, you can see most of Jeddo's Run holler, from the woods below Barnes' field almost all the way to Yankee Run. If we raise our eyes from the kitchen sink, we're looking over the woodshed roof and beyond, to the fringe of woods that laps down over the brow of Rex Hill, where, last summer, we lost two heifers.

We've kept cattle in that pasture for years without any escapees, but this time was special. Something spooked them, and in less time than it takes to tell, they were over two gates and a fence and into the woods. It was June, and the witch hazel, sassafras, and spicebush were so dense that in ten steps, the heifers just disappeared. Fear gave them more than their usual speed, and by the time we knew what had happened, they were just gone.

A Little Local History

Tim, our mechanic down in the village, once told us a story about a cow that got loose in the spring of 1972. It was Easter and there was a parade with floats and wagons and three teams of farm horses, and someone got the idea that there should be a cow marching with the 4-H and FFA kids. Actually, three cows were volunteered, and they looked wonderful sashaying along behind the Buckeye Broncos float right up until they reached the Dairy Isle, and then someone threw lighted black cats* into the street and those cows lit out for distant parts.

left photo by Landon Troyer Photography

Two of them were caught after just a couple of blocks—dairy cows aren't made for speed—but somehow the third one got away. She just disappeared, down an alley, maybe, and no amount of searching could turn her up. She must have made it to the woods along the river, though, because a week later two men fishing at the head of Brown's Island caught sight of her, *swimming* across the river to West Virginia. After they'd caught their limit, they went down to the White Front Cafe and told what they'd saw, and of course nobody believed them because nobody had ever heard of a cow swimming almost a quarter of a mile. But five months later she turned up in New Cumberland, strolling down the sidelines during a highschool football game. They penned her behind the concession stand, and the next day the owner came and fetched her home.

Lost Sheep

With that story in mind, we didn't lose heart when our two Jersey girls flew the coop. After we'd combed the woods without success, we went from door to door all over the length and breadth of Rex Hill. It's mostly just trees on a slope, but there are three twisty lanes and about twenty-five houses; we knocked on doors, talked to people, and left notes where there was no one home. Folks thought it was kind of funny to hear of cows so close to the village, but they took down our number and promised to call if they saw anything.

It was an interesting thing that here we had lived for more than a quarter of a century less than half a mile from most of these folks and had never met them. But there's no straight road up our hill; the county road that used to cut through the home pasture was relocated so long ago that the grass grows thick in the old roadway and our cows make milk out of it. The woods are so steep that few folks ever venture in, and Yankee Road, which used to be the lane folks on the hill took down to the grocery store, has beech trees over two feet in

diameter growing right in the middle. People who want to get down to the village use the blacktop county road and drive fast.

We met Uvalde, whose house just above our farm first belonged to his great-aunt back when black folks weren't welcome to live in the village. He promised to pray for the heifers' speedy return, and so did Carl, who lives in a trailer up by the radio towers and took out his phone to show us before-and-after pictures of his spinal surgery. Reverend Bob was patching concrete in his driveway and had to find his hearing aids before we could tell him what we were looking for, but he turned out to be the biggest help, calling us when the heifers were spotted and acting as traffic cop while the neighbors watched us round them up.

It wasn't all that easy. The heifers were jittery; we couldn't get close, and there was not one fenced yard to hold them while we thought about it. Then the boys had the idea of bringing up one of the mama cows from the farm. They ran home, loaded Delphinium into the trailer, and brought her up. That did it! The moment those heifers caught sight of Delphi, they just about laid down and cried; they were so glad to see her. They loaded right up, and in the end we got them home. Now they wear collars with bells, so if ever they get

photo by Landon Troyer Photography

into the woods again, we'll have some chance of finding them.

The Road Home

Looking out now through the kitchen window, it's hard to believe those woods were ever too dense to penetrate. A few months can make a lot of difference. Today black tree trunks make stripes against a background of snow, and a red fox who dens under the big fallen oak shows up like a dropped mitten. Deer stepping delicately down the steep hillside in search of windfall apples are easily counted, seven white-tailed does and four fawns. Crows in a sycamore look like a line of straggling quarter notes, marking a silent tune against the pearly evening sky.

After the heifers came home, we baked cookies for our neighbors up on Rex Hill, taking them around one Saturday when folks would be home. Children asked how the cows were doing; their escape and recapture had figured as an event in the summer. We got some joshing from older folks who still thought it was funny that we keep cows, especially dairy cows, on a little farm in the woods, but it was all good-natured. In that short time, we had become known to one another.

When darkness falls, we'll see Uvalde's porch light through the trees on the ridge, and to the west, sometimes there's a light in the Wilsons' back window. It's nice that now we have names to go with them. When the Kreugers' husky got loose and came down through the woods to visit our chickens, we knew whom to call.

Today, in January, the woods are wide open. Next June, when the spicebush and sassafras are leafed out and we can't see ten feet, we'll still know the way up the hill. Then if anything wanders off the farm, we'll get it back—especially now that the heifers are wearing bells. 🐔

---

*a brand of fireworks

FAMILY ROOTS

Words by: Shawn & Beth Dougherty
Originally published in September, 2023

COUNTRY LIFE IS ROOTED—tied to the soil, tied to place and family. When you're dependent on your land to feed you, when the soil and the livestock depend on you to care for and feed them, and when all the people on the land share responsibility for this mutual stewardship, life tends to be centered, focused, quite literally *grounded*. When the family sits down to supper together after a busy, sweaty harvest day, they relax into a deep sense of belonging.

Rootedness is very much on our minds when we think of our friends Daniel and Carlee Russell. Because their family—three biological and five adopted children—seem to be a living example of the kind of rooted community that can arise so blessedly out of farm life.

Human Failings

Sometimes a home breaks up over other things than lack of love. It's tragically common: drugs, a growing addiction, episodes of risk for children left without adult care, until finally the community steps in. The goal is to protect the helpless, but sometimes, in almost the ultimate tragedy, siblings are taken from their home piecemeal. Relieved of the fear of bodily harm, they must now face separation from one another.

It was like that for the three Smith children. Taken from their mother's home at ages two and four, Grace and Lia were placed in foster care while their baby brother was left in his mother's custody. Even at age five, Grace knew that her mother's addiction would not allow her to care for Jeb. Later, when he was placed in foster care, it was not in the same

left photo by Landon Troyer Photography

home with his sisters. Although they were now safe and well cared for, the children were still lost, separated from one another.

Second Chances

Then Carlee and Daniel came into the picture.

The Russell home has been a refuge since the beginning of their marriage. A full-time youth pastor, Daniel knows what lost and confused looks like, and he's got a vocation for helping. Most importantly, he knows that life is a work in progress. "The goal of ministry isn't to keep people from making mistakes," he says. "It's to give them tools for conversion, and to model conversion."

"Life is a day-to-day decision," adds Carlee. "To consider ourselves failures is to put God on a timeline."

The couple's choice to serve in foreign mission work during university morphed into youth ministry and domestic hospitality when they married. Although complications in pregnancy limited their biological children to three, the Russells prayed for a large family—and God answered their prayers. "There was usually someone living with us," says Carlee. "A single mother, a family whose house burned, a college student—we always had someone to love on." Later, when the children got older and began leaving for college, a new opportunity for domestic ministry opened up.

One day, a friend told Carlee about three small Native American siblings who had been separated in foster care. Carlee felt sure she was hearing a call from God. "I went home and told Daniel, 'I think we're supposed to take them.'" Many couples, with their own children nearly grown, might have been looking forward to a new chapter of married life without small children, but Daniel didn't hesitate. "Let's do it," he told Carlee.

Obstacles were ignored. Fast-tracking their foster parent training, the Russells requested custody of the three Smith children, and within two months the siblings were united on the family's beautiful Wyoming homestead.

It was a new beginning. The children were together, secure from want or harm. They were with loving, responsible adults. They had regular meals and clean clothes. Their school attendance was consistent. They enjoyed a vibrant farm life: outdoor play, gardening, animal care. And when Carlee and Daniel were granted permanent legal guardianship (Native American children cannot be formally adopted by non-Native Americans), the siblings knew this was their forever home.

Putting Down Roots

Farm life was more than agreeable to the three young Smith—now Russell—children; it was a taste of Heaven.

A small farm is a great place to get to know God—you can see His creatures up close, with no distractions: the miracle that cows can eat grass, and turn it into milk every day to feed babies—calf or human; the wonder of a baby chick hatching, pipping its way through its eggshell with the tiny "egg tooth" on its beak; the blue of a robin's egg. In the garden, God's provision is everywhere, tiny seeds miraculously becoming scarlet beets, sweet corn, watermelons. Roots go deep; security literally flows from the earth.

The children's human roots were being cared for, too. They had regular video conversations with their birth mother. Daniel and Carlee were deliberate about keeping the children in contact with their extended birth family, even taking vacations with the Smith grandparents, who live nearby. The children had cousins in their classes at school. Life took on a new security.

But when they became aware that their mother, now living in a different state, was expecting another child, suddenly their world was destabilized. Grace, the oldest, was almost overwhelmed with concern that the new baby would experience the same risk and neglect she and her brother and sister

had known. Now seven years old, she felt a strong sense of responsibility for her unborn sibling. She couldn't be comfortable until Carlee and Daniel had promised that they would be ready, if the chance ever came, to take the baby in.

Not One Sparrow

Baby Bryn was born early in 2021, but to the Russells' disappointment, she was not placed in their care. So, when Carlee and Daniel learned that the children's mother was expecting a fifth child, they kept the information from the three siblings. "We knew how much they would worry," says Carlee. Born six weeks prematurely, the new baby, Annie, went directly with Bryn into foster care. Uniting all five siblings now looked less possible than ever. And then one evening, there came a phone call; would the Russells take the two babies in?

"We got the paperwork underway just as fast as possible," Carlee recounts. "The girls were 15 hours away. We bought two new car seats and set out in the middle of the night, without knowing whether we would get the babies or not."

Coming to Land

The morning when Bryn and Annie met their older siblings will always live in the family's memory. For the two oldest girls, life changed forever. Worry became delight as they held their little sisters. "I saw the weight of the world fall from their shoulders," Carlee recalls. Jeb, once the youngest, became an instant older brother; half jealous, half protective.

The storms of life can tear a family to pieces; it happens only rarely that everyone washes up on the same shore. Today the young Russells are abundantly blessed and thriving. They work with Carlee in the garden, help Daniel gentle a young steer. At school, they are making good progress; last spring, Lia even won a state-wide coloring contest. Life is good.

Grace puts the experience into words: "I'm so glad you are my family," she says. 🐦

SERIOUS ABOUT FOOD

Words by: Shawn & Beth Dougherty
Originally published in November, 2023

TO SOME PEOPLE, our farm looks like a hobby. For us to spend so much time, thought, and energy just growing *food* seems peculiar—almost disproportionate. After all, there's a Walmart just fifteen miles away. Food is cheap; food is easy. What's so wonderful about growing it yourself?

This seems to us a funny question considering that food has been the primary consideration of all humankind almost since Creation. Home-grown food is fresher, we might point out, and you can choose to grow it without questionable chemicals. It comes from the shortest possible supply chain, so it's hard to interrupt. It's powered by local sunlight. And, to paraphrase James Rebanks, working together makes us who we are; it makes us belong.

Provision

Putting up a year's worth of food doesn't happen in a rush; it's something that's planned out, with projects initiated months, or even years, ahead of need. Seeds take time to sprout, grow, and bear fruit; animals require time, room, and calories to grow. Goals must be set for production, and plans made for food preservation and storage. Many factors need to be synchronized.

If you're serious about growing your food, you're not leaving anything to chance. Fortunately, whole-diet provisioning follows a traditional pattern—one that, although it varies from farm to farm and climate to climate, has generally similar outlines almost everywhere.

Energy

The first crop in any food production plan is the staple crop.

Staple foods are the carbohydrates we eat often, even several times a day. In the U.S., this is usually wheat; in other parts of the world it might be rice, corn, millet, or some other starchy food. Our family's staple is potatoes, partly because they are easy to grow, harvest, and store, and partly because we love them. It's not uncommon to see potatoes on our table three times a day. So, we grow a lot of potatoes every year—a ton or more. We plan to grow even more than we need—in case the crop doesn't do well.

The need for a backup crop isn't just theoretical! Once, we lost the whole potato crop to late blight, the disease that caused the Irish Potato Famine. Two thousand pounds of potatoes turned black and rotted in three days. We were glad we weren't dependent on our potatoes to survive, at least not yet; there's a grocery store in the village just down the road. But store potatoes are of unknown quality; and store potatoes might not always be there. After the blight year, in addition to our potato crop, we grew large back-up crops of corn, beans, and winter squash, just to be sure of our year's calories.

Variety

Our gardens are pretty big—all told, they cover about an acre—and we grow all the vegetables and fruits we enjoy. Kentucky Wonder green beans bunch alongside trellises of Amish Paste tomatoes; giant Tromboncino squash clamber over the garden fence. Rows of onions and garlic march between beds of Detroit Dark Red beets and Danvers Half-Long carrots, and ruffles of Buttercrunch lettuce and Bloomsdale Long-Standing spinach edge the garden paths. There are forests of Country Gentleman corn and Jerusalem artichokes.

We have a big berry patch alongside our kitchen garden where strawberries, gooseberries, raspberries, and blackberries grow. In the middle of the patch we've planted hazelnuts, and it looks like this year we'll get a crop. Chinese chestnuts grow along the creek in the bottom pasture; the woods are full of beech trees. And the farm has many apple trees; some were here before we came, and we have planted more.

Savory

Absolutely the biggest crop on the farm—and the easiest one to grow—is grass. It grows whether you want it to or not. It's out there catching our sunlight and locking it down from early spring to late in the fall; some even grows in the winter.

There are plant species in our fields and pastures for every kind of weather pattern, every kind of nutritional need. Harvesting our grass is the most important job we do all year because it's our most reliable source of energy, year-round.

But of course, we can't eat grass—so we partner with animals that can.

Thanks to our dairy cows, fresh milk comes into the kitchen morning and evening, and even with only five of us in the house, we go through a couple of gallons every day. Yogurt, kefir, and buttermilk are probiotic super-foods, but we consume them just because we like them. There's butter and cheese, of course, both easy to make and easy to store; they keep just fine in the cellar, no refrigeration necessary.

It's like a miracle: pasture plants, when eaten by a cow, sheep, or goat, become the highest quality and most delicious proteins and fats we can imagine. What our gardens can't provide, our cows and sheep can make—from just plain grass.

Plenty

If it sounds like we grow a lot of food, we do! When you seriously set out to provide for your family, you plan to grow extra, and most years there is far more than you can eat—a generous surplus. On some farms this would be sold, but here, most is put to more traditional uses.

Pigs are a farm's natural surplus-converters—partner animals that turn spare calories of every kind into portable, reproducible, non-electric, stored-on-the-hoof bacon and pork chops. Before refrigeration and cheap long-distance transportation, traditional food storage was spelled P-I-G. Our pigs' appetites are in our thoughts when we plan our garden: we grow plenty of everything, knowing that any extra has a future as ham and sausage.

Surplus dairy products have the same destiny. A dairy cow or two giving you six to eight gallons of milk a day at the peak of their production might be overwhelming, but not if you've got a pig in the barn. All that extra skim milk or buttermilk, and whey from cheese-making, are welcome additions to a piggy diet. In fact, milk-fed pigs make the best pork; and by keeping our food and feed needs on-farm, we know what is in our food, and we know it will be there.

Even our poultry have a job to do. Chickens graze buckwheat and turnips in the gardens, adding fertility and organic matter to beds that, next year, will be used for people crops. Corn, sorghum, sunflower seeds, and fodder beets ('mangel-wurzels') supplement their food ration, along with skim milk (yes, chickens drink milk!) for extra protein. Food and butchering scraps also boost egg production.

Security

By November, the cellars are full of potatoes, beets, and winter squash, and there is cheese in the cheese cave. Jars of salsa, green beans, apple slices, dried fruit, and jam line the basement shelves. In the smokehouse hang sides of bacon and hams. Ropes of onions and garlic dangle from pegs in the cellar, and the freezers are full of beef and pork from the fall butchering.

Summer, with its long, warm, sunny days, was our opportunity to work together to harvest energy for the dark, cold winters, and we have not wasted our time. 🐦

Homestead Living

with MELISSA K. NORRIS

Melissa K. Norris is a 5th generation homesteader who married a city boy... but that city boy quickly became a country boy and turned into a bon-afide farmer when they moved to Melissa's family property. With their two children, they believe in keeping the old ways alive. She is an author, blogger, and podcaster. Learn more by visiting: www.melissaknorris.com.

Words by: Melissa K. Norris
Originally published in January, 2023

Welcome to My Homestead

SOME OF MY EARLIEST MEMORIES are of planting beans in the vegetable garden behind our white 1974 single-wide trailer home. My job was to drop the bean into the indent my mother made in the soil, as I was too young to know how deep was necessary.

As years passed, I would plant by myself. In late summer, Dad and I harvested the beans, delivering them to Mom for the stringing and snapping to fill the Mason jars lining the cramped countertops in the kitchen. We pressure-canned the beans to fill the pantry. There was never an August without the punctuation of the pressure canner's hiss and jiggle. I thought it was commonplace that every family raised a garden and put-up food for the winter months.

Growing up, I felt I didn't quite fit in with many of my peers. Instead of preschool, dance lessons, or little league sports, towering evergreens were my playmates, and old-growth, hollowed-out stumps were my forts. Though I am one of ten children, I'm the oldest from my father's second marriage. All of the older kids from his first marriage moved out by the time I was one, and my younger brother wasn't born until I was eleven.

Living rurally, we were lucky to get two channels on TV when there was snow on the mountain. If we turned the antenna attached to the porch just right, the signal bounced off the white-capped peaks, giving us a grainy

picture and audio. Entertaining myself fell to imagination, reading, and the forest outside our trailer.

Laura Ingalls Wilder was my best friend growing up. Every night, my mom would read a chapter to me before bed. We started with *Little House in the Big Woods*. No matter how much I begged, it was a strict one-chapter-a-night rule. (I'm sure she knew if she gave me an inch, we'd be reading until past midnight.)

Once I learned to read on my own, I reread the entire series. If you bend a vine-maple sapling over, straddle it near the top, and push off with your feet, it recoils just enough for you to believe you're riding Pet and Patty with Laura on the trail.

My mom homeschooled me for preschool and kindergarten. A few months into first grade at public school, my teacher knelt and said, "I'm really proud of how well you're doing without having been in school before."

She meant it as a compliment (and to this day remains one of my favorite teachers), but even at six years old, it meant there was a distinction between me and the rest of my classmates. I wasn't the same as them.

My mother sewed many of my clothes. At that time, it was cheaper to sew clothes than it was to buy (though that's no longer the case with the cost of fabric and notions compared to cheap, ready-made items available today). I longed for a store-bought dress so I wouldn't look different than the other kids.

Two life-forming events happened the year I turned eight.

The first: I discovered that one could write books for a living. I vowed I would one day become an author.

The second was when my best friend told me her stepmother said, "I don't know why you want to go to their house. They just live in an old trailer."

My best friend, in anger, relayed the sentence to me. With wisdom far beyond her years, my best friend liked to come to our house because she could feel the warmth and love inside the walls, but my eight-year-old self only knew that some people looked down on our home, and that transferred to looking down on me.

When I reached high school, we moved a half-mile up the road to an older two-story house, and I thought I'd left that trailer behind.

Then I met a boy and when we got married and started our life together, guess where we ended up. Yep, right back in that 1974 single-wide trailer.

Though I grew up living close to the land, as a newlywed who worked a day job, I discovered why convenience foods became popular in the

"Two life-forming events happened the year I turned eight. The first: I discovered that one could write books for a living. I vowed I would one day become an author."

first place. Because they're convenient. When you don't walk through the door until 6pm or later, it's hard to put a completely from-scratch home-cooked meal on the table.

But convenience comes at a cost. After the birth of my second child—my daughter—the heartburn I'd experienced with both pregnancies didn't recede as it did after having my son.

It got worse; a lot worse. I took prescription medications up to six times a day, and it still didn't control the acid. At twenty-nine years old, I checked into the hospital for an endoscope. While I was out, they performed a biopsy on my upper stomach and esophagus for cancer.

Thankfully, it came back negative, but the results showed erosion and cellular change. The specialist told me, "You should never have been allowed to be on these doses or these medications for this long. You must figure out a way to control the acid by the foods that you eat, or the next time you come in, you won't be this lucky."

A fat stack of papers sat beside my purse on the passenger seat on the long drive home. With each mile, my resolve grew. I knew I had a choice, to figure out a way to control the GERD and acid literally eating away at my stomach, or I likely wouldn't be around to see my babies graduate or dance at their weddings.

I set out on a mission to eliminate all genetically modified ingredients, high fructose corn syrup,

food dyes, MSG, and any ingredient label I couldn't pronounce or didn't know what it was. I turned back to the foods of our forefathers. Real grass-fed butter, lard, and coconut oil. To afford or find versions with ingredients meeting these criteria, we had to grow and make the majority ourselves.

We'd always had a garden, and we'd been raising and canning our green beans and grass-fed beef (because grass was much cheaper than grain). That was the only thing we produced enough of to eat from the entire year.

Quickly, we began to produce 99% of all our meat, from grass-fed, grass-finished beef, pasture-raised pork, meat chickens, and hens for eggs to over 70% of our fruits and vegetables for an entire year for our family of four.

All of this we did while still commuting and working day jobs. Though I had the advantage of watching my mother cook from scratch as a child, I was the first woman in my family who practiced homesteading while working a full-time job away from the homestead.

During this time, not only did I work at the pharmacy, but I also pursued my goal of becoming a published author. I started a blog because I learned publishers no longer sign authors unless they have an online platform.

I was not the only one who sacrificed health on the altar of processed convenience foods, albeit unknowingly. Thousands of others responded to what I shared on my website, seeking to return to a simpler and from-scratch kitchen while still living in

a modern world. My tutorials, recipes, and videos became a bridge.

I've discovered many lessons in the thirty-three years that have passed since I was eight. What a small and sad person who believes someone's worth is tied to the type of home they live in.

You may think I'm referring to the stepmom of my friend, but I'm actually referring to myself.

I never looked down on others who lived in trailers or homes past their prime, but deep down inside, I carried shame, and the embers secretly flared when someone joked about "trailer trash." I unconsciously looked down on myself.

It took decades for me to see the immense value of coming from that trailer. The reason I didn't see our trailer as something undesirable—until that careless comment—was because it was filled with love.

My mom cooked almost every meal in the tiny kitchen. Though we didn't have much by worldly standards, we frequently had extra guests at dinner. The worn table overflowed with simple food, laughter, and tall tales.

Any building can shelter you, but it's the people who fill it that make it a home.

I'm now the author of several books, including my newest, *Everything Worth Preserving.* 🐦

Blessings and Mason jars,

Melissa

Words by: Melissa K. Norris
Originally published in May, 2023

Clover the Cow

DEATH IS NOT something our society is very comfortable talking about. There has been a shift towards avoiding any pain or hardships in recent decades. While I don't purposefully set out to cause myself pain (it's human nature to protect ourselves), it is a fact of life here on earth.

Growing up on a farm, one is more aware of the cycle of life and death. At eight years old, I was the only child still at home (my older seven siblings were adults, and my two younger brothers hadn't been born yet; for those of you who don't know, I'm one of ten children).

Though we had a herd of one hundred and thirty cattle, my father still worked his day job as a log truck driver. When the on-site butcher came, it was my job to show them which cows and steers were being butchered. Obviously, the goal is to only butcher steers, but when using a bull (no AI), you don't get to pick the gender. If we had a year where more females were born than males, that meant some cows would get butchered.

Because I was the only remaining kid at home, I helped my dad feed the herd every evening through fall and winter. I learned to drive a stick shift at eight, even though I could barely get the clutch all the way to the floorboard because my legs were so short. I tell you what, there's no faster way to learn not to pop the clutch than having your dad standing on the tailgate and throwing him off!

Due to the butcher's schedule, they could only come mid-week. Dad couldn't afford to miss a day of hauling, so it was my responsibility to meet the butcher in the field and point out which cows were to be harvested.

Dad went through the list with me the night before, "The two-year-old bald face steer with the red mark above his eye, the one with the horns, and the curled-hoof cow."

We didn't have numbered ear tags. Dad knew each cow, how many calves she'd had, and if she was a good mom or not from being with his herd. Not to mention it was an extra expense we couldn't afford.

When the butcher showed up, I met them in the field. I pointed out each cow according to Dad's list.

The last cow was the curled-hoof one. We waited for the butcher to gut the cows to get the tongues, hearts, and livers (those are taken at butcher time, on-site).

I gasped in horror when they processed the curled-hoof cow. She was carrying an almost full-term calf.

I'd picked the wrong cow.

There were two curled-hoofed cows in the herd. One was pregnant, and the other was not.

Hot tears burned my eyes. Sorrow gripped my chest in an iron grip.

With the advent of social media, I've seen many a person claim if you raise animals for meat, you're heartless and cruel. Most of these folks haven't a clue about what a farmer goes through.

We care deeply about our animals. We understand sacrifice. I'd dare to say we understand it at a level someone who has only bought their food from a grocery store never will.

We sacrifice under the hot days of summer when hay must be brought in. When our skin glistens not with the drops from a sprinkler or quick

dip in the creek but from sweat and bits of itchy hay. In winter, we're breaking ice, draining hoses, and feeding extra portions, multiple times a day.

When an animal is sick or in trouble, we will stay up all night, in any weather, to nurse it back. We cry when they don't make it and rejoice when they do.

This past January, we battled for a full week to save our milk cow, Clover. She birthed a breech, upside-down, large bull calf. For two days, we were out every four hours, in the wee pitch-black hours of the morning and the cold sleeting hours of the afternoon, fighting to keep her alive.

She was buried in our back pasture on a Friday afternoon. For the next 24 hours, I cried almost non-stop. Her death hit me harder than any other animal we've shepherded in my forty-two years of farm life.

> "But isn't that the beauty of redemption? Even when something is hard. Painful. It doesn't seem to make sense... until redemption."

I am a day late turning in this article because, though I felt God nudging me to share this story with you, my heart didn't want to relive it in the telling.

In the moment, I wasn't sure why God had brought Clover into our lives only to have her exit what felt so prematurely. We'd only had her for nine months.

But isn't that the beauty of redemption?

Even when something is hard. Painful. It doesn't seem to make sense... until redemption.

We're going to have pain in this life. We live in a broken world.

We cannot change that fact. No matter how much we want to or how hard we try.

But God can take those broken circumstances and, from the ashes, create beauty.

If we'd not had Clover go down and require the use of hip clamps, I wouldn't have put out the SOS call on social media to locate a pair. Which means I'd have never met the lovely dairy farmer and her husband who came to the rescue of complete strangers on a dark January night.

We've since become friends and are now attending a Bible study together. I know we've yet to see all God will bring from our having met.

Redemption means despite all the things I've done wrong in my life—and there are many—God forgave them. Not only does that mean I get to go to heaven someday to be in His presence, but He's actively redeeming situations in my life here on earth. And yours, too.

As I thought of a recipe to share with you here, I couldn't find one more fitting than this.

My great-grandmother passed down many things in our family, and though I never knew her, I still think of the woman she was whenever I use her recipes or sieve while making applesauce, raspberry jelly, and blackberry syrup.

I know she was a God-fearing woman and an excellent baker, hence her recipe for Heavenly Chocolate Mayo Cake is still our go-to recipe. I wonder if she had any idea her legacy would live on in my home. 🐦

Blessings and Mason jars,
Melissa

Grandma's Chocolate Mayo Cake & Caramel Frosting

Cake Ingredients

- 2 cups flour (I use fresh ground soft white wheat, but all-purpose or cake flour is fine.)
- 1 cup sugar
- 1/2 cup cocoa
- 1 teaspoon baking soda
- 1 teaspoon baking powder
- 3/4 cup mayonnaise
- 1/2 cup cold water
- 1/2 cup brewed coffee
- 1 teaspoon vanilla

Frosting Ingredients

- 5 Tablespoons butter
- 1 and 1/2 cups brown sugar
- 3 Tablespoons boiling water
- 1 teaspoon vanilla

Instructions

1. Preheat oven to 350 degrees. Stir all dry ingredients together. Combine wet ingredients with dry until smooth. Pour into greased and floured pans. Bake at 350 degrees for 30 to 40 minutes for a cake or 16 minutes for cupcakes. Cool completely before frosting.

2. For frosting, beat butter and vanilla together. Slowly add in sugar until creamed together. Pour in boiling water and beat until creamy. Spread over cake/cupcakes.

Words by: Melissa K. Norris
Originally published in October, 2023

Pumpkin Roll Memories

I'VE BEEN A COLLECTOR OF RECIPES since I was a little girl. When I was eight years old, I walked up our country road to the log cabin a few houses down and knocked on the door, asking Joann if I could have her recipe for the rhubarb dessert she'd shared with our family the night before. I still make it to this day.

Certain foods are forever tied to specific people and memories. The older I get, the more of these connections I have. While some dishes remind us of Thanksgiving, Christmas, and Easter, there are many that remind us of the people who first made them for us.

Such is my story with pumpkin rolls. I've never been a fan of pumpkin pie. I love pumpkin bars, pumpkin cheesecake, and pumpkin spice, but a pumpkin pie, eh, I can take it or leave it. But on the first Thanksgiving spent with my husband's family, I discovered a new pumpkin delight: Grandma's pumpkin roll. It's the perfect marriage of cheesecake and moist pumpkin cake rolled into one. I may have had two... or three helpings. I later learned Grandma had standing orders around the holidays of people wanting her pumpkin roll.

In the past, I'd tried some of Grandma's recipes, only to have my husband tell me, "It's not how Grandma's tasted." You can imagine how well that went over. I called up Grandma and asked if I could come down

and have her teach me how to make her pumpkin roll. One rainy afternoon, I packed up the kids and headed to the next town over for my baking lesson. A few hours later, we'd lined the countertop with three perfect pumpkin rolls. And I became the official holiday family maker of pumpkin rolls from there on out.

I've made them for bake sale fundraisers over the years, and just this week someone asked if they could buy one from me this holiday season even if it wasn't for a fundraiser, as it was the best they'd ever had.

This coming holiday season is the first without Grandma. She passed away this summer. Yet every time I bake her pumpkin roll, she lives on. There is something beautiful to be said of a legacy left in the foods that continue to feed our families. It's not one that can be found with thawing or setting out a store-bought pie. It's found in the art of creation—of the time spent crafting something by hand for those we love.

You can use store-bought canned pumpkin, but this truly tastes best with fresh pumpkin. You can roast it in the oven or do a quick version where you cook it whole in the Instant Pot. Place a whole pumpkin in the Instant pot, use a knife to pierce the skin in a few spots so steam can escape as it's cooking, add a cup of water, and cook on high pressure for 15 minutes. Release the pressure, allow it to cool, remove pumpkin. Cut the pumpkin in half, scoop out the seeds, separate the cooked pumpkin from the skin. Puree until smooth (you may need to add a touch of water to the blender or food processor to make puree smooth).

Blessings and Mason jars,

Melissa

Pumpkin Roll Recipe from Grandma with Fresh Pumpkin

(shared from my book Hand Made: the Modern Guide to Made-from-Scratch Living)

Ingredients

- 3 eggs well-beaten
- 1 cup sugar
- ⅔ cup cooked pumpkin
- ¾ cup flour
- 1 teaspoon baking powder
- ½ teaspoon salt
- ½ teaspoon ground nutmeg
- 1 ½ teaspoons ground cinnamon
- ½ teaspoon ground ginger

Grandma's Notes: Beat for 5 minutes until light and foamy

Filling

- 1 cup powdered sugar *+ more for sprinkling the towel*
- 8 ounces cream cheese
- ½ cup butter softened
- 1 teaspoon vanilla extract
- 2 teaspoons maple syrup, optional

Instructions

1. Preheat oven to 375° Fahrenheit.

2. Grease and flour a 15×10-inch jelly roll pan with coconut oil and be generous with your grease.

3. Mix together flour, baking powder, salt, and spices. Beat eggs for 5 minutes (yes, the whole 5 minutes) until light and foamy, cream in sugar and cooked pumpkin. Then stir in dry ingredients until combined.

4. Pour into prepared jelly roll pan and spread until even. Pick up the pan and tap it (the bottom of the pan) against the counter a few times, this makes the air bubbles rise out of the batter. (I jumped when Grandma did this, it makes a bang!)

5. Bake for 13 to 15 minutes, until the cake is done. Place a clean flour sack or tea towel on the counter and sprinkle with a bit of powdered sugar.

6. As soon as the cake comes out of the oven, run a butter knife around the outside edge of the cake to separate it from the pan. Immediately, using hot pads—that cake is hot—turn the pan upside down over the prepared towel.

7. As soon as cake is out of the pan, place another clean flour sack towel on the short end of the cake and roll up like a sleeping bag. Cool on a wire rack for about 30 minutes. *see photo on left*

8. Prepare your filling by creaming together the cream cheese, powdered sugar, softened butter, vanilla, and maple syrup. Unroll cooled cake and smear the filling evenly over the surface. Reroll the cake, cover, and allow to chill in fridge. Before serving, sprinkle with powdered sugar if desired.

EXTRA TIP: You can make this easy pumpkin roll recipe and freeze it ahead of time! Simply thaw overnight in the fridge before serving.

Connecting Family

with MARK GREGSTON

Mark has spent the last 40 years dedicating his efforts to helping teens and families as a Young Life Area Director, youth pastor, and for the last 35 years, as a director of Heartlight, a residential ministry and counseling center for teens and their families. Since its inception, Heartlight has been home to over 3,000 young people. Mark is a popular speaker, author, and radio host with a profound dedication to helping families stay connected. He and his wife, Jan, call Hallsville, Texas home. You can find out more about Mark, his work with teens, and all his parenting resources at ParentingTodaysTeens.org.

LEND ME YOUR EAR

Words by: Mark Gregston

Originally published in August, 2023

. . . .

IF THERE WAS SOME ACTION that you could take that might change the destiny of your family... would you take it?

If there was something that you could do to make everyone in your family feel a sense of value and importance... would you do it?

If you could take hold of the hearts of your kids, your spouse, your parents, or your neighbors and let them know of your love for them, just by doing one thing... would you grab it?

And, if you had the ability to create an atmosphere where YOU would be heard... are you willing to take a chance to make that happen?

Here it is... that one simple but hard, easy but difficult, and challenging "thing" is this: Listen.

I have spent my life working with teens, meeting with their families, and helping parents connect and reconnect with their family members. I live with 60 high school kids at the Heartlight program that my wife, Jan, and I started 35 years ago; a haven of hope for struggling teens. It's really become a place of restoration for thousands of families since its inception, and I've met with thousands of moms and dads, teens, and even grandparents along the way—helping them learn that one thing could "change it all"... learning to listen.

We live in a world where people have quit listening to one another because they're so busy and caught up in the minutia of life that they spend more time "spouting" than they do actually trying to hear what the other person is saying and wanting to communicate.

I see this over and over in the lives of families. The common denominator of "not listening" to one another trumps

> "We live in a world where people have quit listening to one another ... they spend more time 'spouting' than they do actually trying to hear what the other person is saying..."

the opportunity for connection, thus the conduit for the transfer of wisdom, family values, and beliefs gets broken and there's barely a trickle of wisdom that waters the heart with hope and understanding.

This has been shown to me in several ways.

A wife who has learned that it's better to keep her mouth shut than take a chance of communicating true thoughts and ideas.

A husband who gives up and retreats from conversations because he's tired of not being listened to when he shares the values that have made him the man that he is.

A son who rebels, starts acting out, and looks "elsewhere" for that listening ear. He gives up any religious training or upbringing in hopes of finding

that "one special ear" that is concerned (and interested) in his heart.

A daughter who abandons any hope of a relationship with a mom or dad who loves her dearly because of a feeling that her words spoken from her heart don't really mean anything to those she cares for.

A grandparent who is ignored but longs to share their life stories with family so that traditions and values can be passed on and wisdom gathered through a lifetime of experiences can be shared.

We all see the need. And if we could just quit doing "some things" then the door would be open for this trait of "listening" to rise to the top and become a character trait that creates the atmosphere for the listener to be heard. That's right. Become the greatest listener, and you'll become one that all want to hear from.

Here are some habits that keep listening from happening. You should think about and determine if some of these conducts and behaviors are things that you do to prevent those around you from being heard.

INTERRUPTING. Are you one who can't wait for someone to finish sharing their thoughts so you can jump in with your comments, cutting off others, and basically saying, *"Your thoughts don't matter... but mine do!"* This is a killer of conversations. Remember the scripture, *"Consider others to be more important than yourself."* It will change the way you listen.

LISTENING TO REPLY, NOT TO UNDERSTAND. Are you the type that spends more time thinking about what you're going to say next rather than hearing, and understanding, what the other is saying? Take your time. Listen fully. And then respond.

BEING A KNOW IT ALL. If you already know everything, then there's really no need for you to have a discussion with anyone... you already know it all. Remember the proverb, *"Even a fool appears wise when they keep their mouth shut."* You may know a lot, so spend time getting to know the one who is sharing with you.

ALWAYS TEACHING A LESSON. Some parents feel that in every teachable moment, there needs to be a lesson. That's not true. I'm not saying you shouldn't be "training up a child," but you might want to consider spreading those lessons out. A child, of any age, needs a listener far more than they need someone who is always teaching the "next lesson."

TRYING TO FIX EVERYTHING. Dads usually do this quite a bit. Just as women are wired to talk, men are wired to fix things. And sometimes we feel that the need to "fix" is more important than just listening to what's being said. If you're like me, I'm always looking for the answer and feel the need to fix everything immediately. A couple of months ago, as I was listening (so I thought) to my wife sharing, I jumped up to give her the "answer." She said this to me: *"Mark, I really don't need you to fix this... I just wanted you to listen to me."* Enough said.

If you carry one of these traits, you might want to double-check and make sure they're not getting in the way of connecting communication within your home. You may be missing something and not even know it. *"Lord, search me, and see if there are any hurtful ways..."*

Those behaviors that you don't like seeing in those around you might just be a response to something that you are doing that's not giving them the ear that they long to have. And if that

loved one around you is struggling, remember that the behavior you see is the visible expression of the invisible issue in their life. They may just want someone to listen to them. And that person might just be you.

So do this: do some self-reflection. Determine if there is a need for you to be a better listener. And if you don't really know, ask them. There's no harm or love lost in asking family members about how you come across. It might just open the door for them to start sharing the deeper things about their life, about how they feel, and what they think about. Ask them!

If you desire to have deeper relationships with your family, and long for future opportunities to influence those around you, then become to others how you would want them to be to you. You'll learn this: people listen to those who listen to them.

What you'll find is a pathway to deeper relationships, more meaningful conversations, and a connection with those you love that might just last a lifetime. There are those in your family who want you to be the one to lend an ear. Give it a shot. See what happens. And whatever you do... *listen.* 🐦

MAKING IT RIGHT

Words by: Mark Gregston

Originally published in September, 2023

. . . .

I'VE SPENT MY LIFE WITH TEENS and their families. It all started 50 years ago when I was 19. A father asked me if I would help with his son who was struggling a bit. That started a lifetime of being a youth pastor and Area Director for Young Life, and for the last 35 years, living with 60 different teens per year at our Heartlight residential counseling program that my wife and I started in Longview, Texas; the place that I call home. It's been a lifetime of helping parents and teens restore that which has been damaged and bringing broken relationships back together.

Recently, I was speaking in a Midwest city, and after I finished, a man I recognized immediately came up to me with tears in his eyes and a heaviness on his heart. His trembling voice spoke these words: *"I need to ask your forgiveness."* It was the first thing I'd heard from him in four decades. He went on to say how angry he was with me when I asked him and his wife to move out of our house where we had temporarily let them live. His message was simple but so difficult for him to say. It was a simple message that took forty years of building up courage to say two small words: *"I'm sorry."*

We hugged with my explanation that I had sold the house, thus terminating our offer of giving them free rent. He had been "stewing" over that situation all this time, resulting in forty years of no contact, no words, and sadly, no relationship. Not exactly a picture of the scripture that reminds us to not let the sun go down on our anger.

I've seen this hundreds of times, if not thousands: unre-solved conflict that lingers. It damages relationships. And those

unresolved issues have a weird way of coming to the surface at a later time, usually at significant life events with greater consequences affecting a larger circle of relationships.

But it does more than that. The choice to keep issues "unresolved" keeps all from experiencing the benefit of those relationships that God has placed in our lives, thus, never experiencing the deeper relationship He intended. Just one person's choice, negative or positive, can have an impact on family members, children, neighbors, and others within communities. Sadly, many choose to remain in the shallow end of relationships.

My encouragement to all is this: *Make it right.*

Many choose to "not resolve" and believe that this tact is far better than resolving conflict. It's a choice based in fear of not knowing what to do, or, feeling it's better to "hold onto the conflict"

as if to take control over another. Both choices of neglect are simply selfish and hardly fulfill the scripture to "consider others to be more important than yourself."

MOMS AND DADS. There isn't a parent I know who doesn't have conflict with their teens. It's normal to have disagreements, as conflict is a precursor to change. Here're some things that might need to be a starting point to some very important dinner discussions:

An admission of mistakes that shows your authenticity and genuineness; two traits of deep relationships.

Disclosure of statements that you've made that have hurt your relationship and those skirmishes that have never been resolved.

Divulging your own issues and struggles that show your humility and humanness. Your teens

> **"The choice to keep issues 'unresolved' keeps all from experiencing the benefit of those relationships that God has placed in our lives, thus, never experiencing the deeper relationship He intended."**

just might have a fond affection to your display of authenticity and show of faithfulness to the relationship that you have with them. And you might even set an example where they'll begin to share the battles they encounter.

Your child is hoping you'll affirm your relationship with them by letting them know that there's nothing they can do to make you love them more, and nothing they can do to make you love them less. And by talking about those things that are getting in the way of your relationship, you are opening the door to a deeper relationship.

Today may be the day. Make it right.

HUSBANDS AND WIVES. You've committed your life to one another. If you let it, the unresolved conflict in your marriage will eventually destroy your relationship if you don't act to "tear down the walls" as quickly as they are "constructed." Jan and I have always thought it best to not let the sun go down on our conflicts. And that has meant some very real and direct talks, late at night, and the admission of something that is so hard for husbands and wives to say. "I'm sorry."

Before you go to sleep at night... make it right.

GRANDPARENTS. You are the backbone of your family. Your redemption of any time lost to conflict and struggle can be an example. You're probably in the 4th quarter of life. The value of your legacy will not be measured by the amount you've left in your kid's or grandkid's bank account. It will be measured by what you have deposited in their heart. So, take advantage of the crucial time. This may be a time to restore what's been lost, to make sure there are no skeletons left in the closet to scare your kin in the days ahead, and to "clear the air" with relationships within your family. And it can begin as easily as these comments shared with family.

"I want you to know that I'm not perfect and I've done some things I'm not proud of. I'd like to share these with you so you don't hear them from anyone else after I'm gone."

"Hey, there're some issues I need to share about our family that haven't been talked about. I think it's important for you to know so your family can learn from our mistakes."

"I hope we can have a frank discussion about some things I've learned about life so that you don't have to go through the pain I experienced to learn the same lessons."

Your family wants to talk about the things that haven't been talked about, no matter how hard it is to bring certain topics up for discussion. It may be the time to start making some of those statements that open the door to deepen all your relationships within your family.

Make it right. While there's still time.

I've said this for years: *"I can always make more money, but I can't make more time."* My encouragement to you is that you would take advantage of the time, and "make it right" with those around you. Redeem the time that's been lost.

Ask to get together. Speak the truth with calmness, love, and grace. Be quick to listen, slow to speak, and slow to anger when you hear their feelings and responses. And end the conversation hiding nothing and sharing everything. Your actions today might just have an effect on the destiny of your family.

THE MISSION FIELD OF FAMILY

Words by: Mark Gregston

Originally published in November, 2023

· · · · · · · · ·

I'VE HAD WONDERFUL OPPORTUNITIES to visit some amazing countries and spend time on the mission field helping those in need, mainly targeting kids who have been living in orphanages and waiting for adoption. I most recently was in Addis Ababa, Ethiopia where I was able to spend a few days with a group of 200 young girls at an orphanage. No doubt they loved having an older white guy with grey hair hang out with them for a few days. It was the mission trip of a lifetime.

I think I helped a little. Maybe. As I was there, I thought about the cost of the trip—the housing, travel, and meals—and wrestled a bit with the vast amount of dollars it took to get there... just to be on the mission field. Nonetheless, it was a great trip. An eye-opening one. To see the need of these young girls encouraged me to want to help more. In reality, I knew there was very little that got accomplished. Traveling all that way and spending all that money that produced very little (in my eyes) was a bit disheartening. And, that trip didn't prepare me for the situation I would come home to, creating conflicting thoughts.

I live with 60 struggling teens who come from all over the country to live in our residential counseling program called

Mark visiting the Ketchanie Orphanage in Ethiopia

Heartlight. This beautiful place is a haven of peace, a respite of hope, and a mission to parents and their struggling teens. But something happened not 400 yards from our place of hope that still puts a lump in my throat to this day.

A 14-year-old young lady named Kim, who lived near our property in East Texas... only 400 yards from a "respite of hope," had a bad day while I was in Ethiopia spending time with the girls at the Ketchanie Orphanage. She was so overwhelmed in the midst of her bad day, that she picked up her two little dogs, put them under her arms, and walked out to the railroad tracks and stood there until an oncoming train took her life. Just 400 yards from where I live. Four. Hundred. Yards.

Here I thought that I had to go thousands of miles away to find a mission project, and I missed the very one that lived just a short distance away. I felt I had missed a chance to help a neighbor.

Last weekend, Jan and I drove to Tulsa, Oklahoma to visit her recently widowed Dad. We spent a couple of days cleaning up his yard, trimming trees, cutting branches, scrubbing out gutters, and caught up on yardwork of his once-pristine home landscape. He had focused his efforts for the last five years on taking care of my ill mother-in-law (an absolute jewel!) and

neglected to take care of everything else around him. He's 94, worn out, sad, lonely, and feels a little lost after fulfilling his purpose of taking care of his bride of 73 years.

Shearing bushes, cutting and tearing down trees, bagging leaves, and chain-sawing remnants of trees that had passed years ago became an act of love for a man who feels much like his yard... neglected, ignored, dying, and in need of some revitalization. This two-day excursion to Tulsa to help my father-in-law is one of the most important mission projects I have ever worked on and been a part of. And it was right there in my family; not a foreign mission that I needed to travel thousands of miles to "help."

I wonder if we all sometimes miss the mission projects right in our own backyard (our family) because we feel that to be "in missions," it's got to be somewhere far away and more exciting.

I wonder if we miss the very "mission" that God has placed in our family, the opportunity to help those who have played a significant part in our lives.

Now don't hear me saying that mission projects should all be at home. Or that we should never travel to help others. What I am saying is that there may be so many people in need right around us, that we don't have to go far to extend them the hand of Christ. The apostle Paul said, *"Share with the Lord's people who are in need. Practice hospitality."* (Romans 12:13)

Your mission field may be right outside your back door. Maybe just 400 yards away. Or someone in your family who desperately needs hope that is wrapped up in a little help.

Would you consider taking on a mission project? It could be someone in your family. Or a neighbor who is within a stone's throw of your porch. Or someone in your church that is too proud to ask for help but needs it more than anyone will ever know. Here are some ideas.

• **Go take care of someone's yard.** When you mow yours, go ahead and mow theirs. When you trim bushes, trim theirs. When you rake leaves, rake theirs. And don't just do it once. Make it a habit to help take care of something that might just mean the world to them.

- **Commit to helping a family that has a child with special needs.** And don't just do it once. Commit to giving them a "break" by saying that you'll be over at their home every Tuesday afternoon for the next 4 years to give them a respite and some time to refresh.
- **Look around you and find a person that looks about as neglected as their home and take on a small project to make life just a little easier for them.** Fix a faucet, help paint a fence, get rid of their garbage. You'd be surprised how small things mean a lot to those who can barely take care of themselves, much less a house, a barn, their property, or anything that once meant the world to them.
- **Instead of keeping your kids from hanging around those "bad" kids, take those kids on as a mission project.** God may have placed those tough kids around you so that you can help change their lives. I've found that these "bad" kids really aren't bad, they're just lost.

And helping someone find their way when they're lost is one of the greatest things anyone can do for another.

There are people around you who are just like the young lady, Kim, who had lost all hope. There are fathers-in-law just like mine who need help but are much too proud to ask for it. Just do it anyway. And there are those who are within a stone's throw of your home and praying for someone just like you to come lend a helping hand.

What I thought was going to be a purposeless, horrible, two-day time of sweating and getting worn out, ended up being my mission project of the year—right in my own family. I've never been thanked so many times as we sat and talked about his wife, getting older, the future, yet-to-be-made decisions about a retirement home, and what to do about a dog that is seeing her last days. God had other plans for my time during those days than what I had thought.

And I was the one that drove home with a sense of fulfillment that my efforts had truly made a difference in the life of one man... right there in my own family. 🐓

Whispers of Hope

with **STACEY GAGNON**

Stacey Gagnon, along with her husband Darren, are the founders of Lost Sparrows. She can be reached at P.O. Box 751, Winona Lake, IN 46590. Learn more about Lost Sparrows at www.lostsparrows.org.

sometimes there is no happy ending...

Words by: Stacey Gagnon

Originally published in April, 2022

I'VE NEVER really talked about him. I guess I wanted to forget, and deep inside, I hoped that the passing of time would fade his story. He was in my home for a shorter time than most of our foster children. He did not reunify with family, he was not adopted, he was not moved to another home. He died.

He died, and when I signed up for foster care, that was definitely not something I felt capable of handling. I mean, seriously, how many of us are capable or willing to bring home a dying child? Looking back, I'm not even sure why I said "yes" when they called about the placement. Naiveté? I guess in my heart I thought he would be like all the other children. He would arrive broken and hurting, and love would fix things. We had experienced some of the most miraculous moments with some critically ill children, and I thought this would be the biggest miracle story of them all. What I had not experienced yet was that sometimes in foster care and adoption, there is no beautiful story of redemption or miracle moment of healing. Sometimes the ending is not happy, and you are sitting, waiting faithfully for God to show up and rescue... and He doesn't.

It was a warm spring night, and I sat in my car in the dark hospital parking lot and sobbed ugly tears. In the seat behind me, I heard flared-nose grunting as the one-year-old pulled in breath after breath. I didn't need to turn around to know that blood mixed with saliva was tracing down his chin, or that his tiny, pearl white teeth were chewing through his bottom lip. In my mind's eye, I saw his wide blue-eyed stare and thick blond curls. I knew his fists would be clenched and his body strung tight as a bow. A survivor of near-drowning, he had been a running, talking, happy toddler just months prior. Now he was called "vegetative" and labeled "DNR" (do not resuscitate).

I heard a voice tauntingly whisper, "You can't save them all." In fact, I had been told that by well-meaning friends when I first agreed to foster him.

Sitting in my car, I was angry and hurt and questioned why God had allowed this to happen. How did God sit by and watch a one-year-old slip beneath the surface of the bathtub water and not fix it? There would be no miraculous healing, no spontaneous return of brain function. This was our third hospital stay in a month, and I had been advised to take him home and stop feeding him. "He only has brain stem function; there's no quality of life." Yet, in my heart, I had believed in a different ending. I honestly believed that God would faithfully step in and heal him. But, medically and scientifically, I knew this wasn't possible, and being discharged by a nurse who tried to explain this to me in "comforting terms" made me angry.

Going into this, I thought I had the resources and the ability. I also thought I understood how this was all supposed to play out. I had signed up to rescue and save; certainly I wasn't being asked to watch a child die because of abuse and neglect. Sitting in that car, I started to ask myself this question: "What if God didn't step in and fix this?" *My God, what if he dies?*

The system had failed. His parents had failed. And I was scared that God had failed also.

I gagged on my sobs and started the car. Medically, I knew he needed surgery and medication. He couldn't keep his airway clear and kept aspirating vomit. Darren and I had not slept for months because we took turns suctioning his airway every time he refluxed and vomited. Nights were scary because at night we held death at bay with a suction machine and pure determination.

I was told that he was not eligible for surgery or the medication because he had been labeled DNR (do not resuscitate) and "that-was-that." But "that-was-that" looks scary and awful when a child is dying in your home beside your bed. "That-was-that" cannot be ignored when a child is chewing through their bottom lip in distress. And my foster child that was just a "brain stem" opened my eyes to a world that places value and worth on intellectual and physical capability; a world that would not allow an animal to die in this manner yet would stand behind three little letters–DNR–and call it justifiable. It had thrust me headlong into brokenness and heartache and gut-wrenching hurt. It was a moment that I felt DNR meant this: Do Not Rescue.

This baby had opened my eyes to a little-known secret: most people don't want to sit in this grief. Most people aren't comfortable watching a baby die, so most people tell you to take them home and stop feeding them, because this is what is humane in their minds. Please take that blonde-haired, blue-eyed chubby baby home and keep that kind of grief to yourself. We sanitize death... we scrub clean the pain and the brokenness because it reminds us of our frailty and the human condition. We don't want to get too close or too personal with suffering. When suffering comes, when death comes, who will bear it with us? Who will see us through it?

Before He died, Jesus wrestled with what He knew was to come. Jesus said to his friends, "My soul is overwhelmed with sorrow, to the point of death" (Matthew 26:38). I take refuge in this. The God of the Universe, the Creator of all things (even those things we call "DNR"), is saying He is overwhelmed with sorrow, even to death...

Death is not easy. For my foster child, there was no silent passing; it was sleepless nights and desperately whispered prayers. And God did not show up in the way that I had begged. Grace and healing did not come on my terms.

He died. But what I learned is that following God means that I am called to get personal with brokenness and suffering. It means accepting that "I can't save them all." In fact, I can't save any; redemption was never my job. My job is to sit in the sorrow, mixed with the blood and saliva of humanity, and desperately whisper my surrender to a throne called GRACE. 🐦

straitjackets and bulletproof vests

Words by: Stacey Gagnon
Originally published in May, 2022

THERE'S WAR in Eastern Europe, and it's very easy to insulate oneself from the realities of living in such violence. It's easy to bury myself in the daily chores of laundry, dishes, and raising children. But my mind won't rest as it keeps reminding me of straitjackets and bulletproof vests.

My first experience in Ukraine was when I flew in as a medical professional to help bring home a very fragile fifteen-year-old named Daniel.

When I went to pick him up, Daniel only weighed 22 pounds. When he left the orphanage, he was wearing a child-sized straitjacket. (*See photo.*)

At birth, he was placed in an institution due to cerebral palsy, and the years of neglect and abuse showed upon his withered frame. His bones pressed against his skin at sharp angles threatening to escape, and his frail body could not hold up his own head. His legs and arms were bent at odd angles as they had grown within the confines of a metal crib. As I carried him onto the plane, I felt his heart flutter against my chest, and his shallow breaths were barely felt on my cheek. I thought he might die

in my arms over the ocean, and I was terrified to carry a dead child off the plane.

We made it to the United States alive. But, while I physically carried a fifteen-year-old boy off the plane and set him into the arms of medical professionals, I did not set down the image of a straitjacket—this article of clothing worn daily by an infant-sized teen boy.

It's much easier to hide these things away. It's easier not to see because seeing these atrocities comes with great cost. And the price is understanding that infant-sized children lie hidden and restrained in orphanages; if I open my eyes to the most vulnerable, I will never be able to unsee this level of darkness.

And yet, the highest form of abuse is indifference. To "not see." To look away from the pain, the dark, the straitjacket.

Which brings me to today. Every part of me wants to look away from the atrocities of war. I want to place my sight upon the daily routine of home and work.

But then I am contacted by a partner of Lost Sparrows, and we are asked to provide bulletproof jackets to protect women and children

> "When I went to pick him up, Daniel only weighed 22 pounds. When he left the orphanage, he was wearing a child-sized straight jacket."

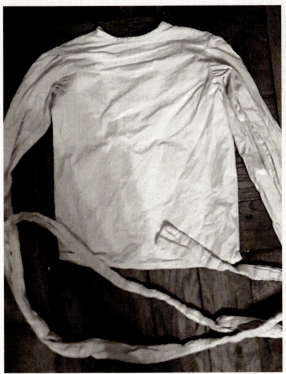

fleeing the violence and bloodshed in Ukraine. The safe "green corridors" are not safe. Innocent women and children are being fired upon in a war that has no regard for the most vulnerable.

And so, my eyes are wide open, and my mind begins figuring out how to get the requests met with our partners in Europe... wound care items, food, medicines... bulletproof vests.

It wasn't until this morning that it all truly hit me. I was cuddling with my six-year-old daughter, Zorey, in her bed filled with warm blankets, soft pillows, and Charlie the stuffed octopus. And I thought of being a mother carrying my child through a war-torn landscape wrapped in a bulletproof vest that, in reality, provides minimal protection. I imagine the cold wind and the press of humanity while I await a ticket to safety. Mumbling prayers with the stark reality that bullets are not meant to tear through the flesh of children, and this vest is too large for my six-year-old.

I might question where the hope is found.

Straitjackets and bulletproof vests are not meant to be worn by children. But I have witnessed this happening, and we must fight the desire to remain insulated, to remain indifferent. Human suffering is everyone's concern. What is needed now is for these victims to know that they are not alone, that they are not forgotten.

And when their bodies cannot walk, we will carry them. When their voices are silenced, we shall speak out for them. And when they are sitting in darkness, we will be there to share our light.

If you'd like to partner with us in Eastern Europe, please consider donating to Lost Sparrows. I also ask that you continue praying. 🐦

lessons from prison

Words by: Stacey Gagnon
Originally published in June, 2022

SHE SAT ACROSS FROM ME, a walking contradiction of motherhood, the embodiment of everything I had spent the last 10 years trying to repair. She represented the mother each of my children had lost when they entered the foster care system. The woman who I feared when we took the foster care training classes. This woman was the unseen specter that hung like a mist within the minds of each of my kids. She was the ghost representing my children's loss of a biological mother.

She sat across from me with her rounded and pregnant belly, the "other woman" I could not forgive.

I judged her, and I felt anger and pain just looking at her.

Her story was a repeat of almost every inmate sitting in their cell: multiple arrests, drug charges, and parole violations. She was a repeat offender with a lengthy rap sheet. But unlike many inmates, she did not deny her guilt. Instead, she wore it on her face and carried it upon her shoulders. I wanted to hate her, I wanted a target to unload upon, and I didn't want her to sit and just take it. I wanted her outrage and denials so that I could howl in my indignant and justified anger.

It was me who had walked the floor with her drug-exposed baby. I held her toddler when he was dropped at my house in a dirty onesie at 2 am.

I watched the first steps, the first gummy grin, the first kiss blown from a chubby palm; and it was me who caught that kiss, that fall, and that broken-hearted child. And this "other woman" was the one who did not.

The "other woman" was wringing her hands, and she looked at me and said, "I want you to tell adoptive parents that I am not what they see on paper. I want them to know that I have done bad things, but I'm not all those things."

I am ashamed that I sat across from her and felt she deserved the pain and anguish she was walking through. I looked at her, and I saw the hours I spent trying to teach her child with the learning disability caused by her alcohol consumption during pregnancy. I saw the day I wiped tears from the five-year-old's eye because he finally understood the word *termination*, a big word that meant he was never going back home to his mommy. I looked, and I calculated the minutes and hours dealing with behaviors steeped in trauma. And inside, I struggled.

I felt like a toddler at that moment, screaming, "MINE." I had fought hard for my children; spent months loving a baby that might leave at any moment; spent nights watching her sleep, tucked in and safe, hoping that judges, case managers, and court officials wouldn't move her on a whim. I supported reunification even though it scared me to the very core, and I had given her child my whole heart, knowing she would probably leave. And now, sitting across from the "other woman," I was slammed with the realization that my adopted children had never been fully "MINE." I didn't know how to reconcile that, and inside I was afraid.

I believe that all adoptive parents carry this unspoken fear of future rejection. Would my children one day stop loving me and start loving the biological mother more? Would I receive a metaphorical pink slip from my child with the words "No longer needed" written in red? I don't want to have these thoughts. I have them anyway.

The "other woman" didn't hand her child over to the surgeon like I did, spending hours pacing the floor waiting to hear if the surgery was a success. She didn't kiss her child's boo-boos, get up in the middle of the night to comfort her during a bad dream, or catch puke in her hands in the back of the van on a family vacation (why do moms try to catch puke in their hands?). In my mind, she did not deserve my child's love.

The "other woman" continued, "I'm broken, but this doesn't mean I don't love my kids. I'd die for my kids. I know what people read about me on paper, but that's not all that I am."

She looked me straight in the eye and said, "They won't let me see my children. They've changed their names, changed their lives... and they have shut me out. But I know my kids will one day want to meet me. I hope they know I'm more than what they've been told. I hope they know I'm not just the bad things I've done, because I love them the best I can. I hope they know that I am a piece of them."

I sat there in my hypocrisy, and I felt sick. As I sat there in the parking lot across from the jail, I gave my hypocrisy to God. The rejection, the fear, and the pain all fell to pieces in my mind because I could not change the past. I could no longer live in the "what-if" or the "could-have-beens."

How could the "other woman" be my enemy? She was a piece of my children. She was the piece that had chocolate brown eyes and thick hair that went on for miles. Her piece was the artistic drawings rendered by my 5th grader and my six-year-old's musical ability. She was the piece that was strong-willed and had a deep love for all small creatures. I realized at that moment that I could

not pick and choose the pieces I deemed bad. No, I had to see all the pieces, and when I look at my children, I see their incredible beauty and potential, and she is a piece of that.

As my children grow, I see that this "other woman" cannot be hermetically sealed within my home. If I don't bring her out into the open, my children will wonder what secrets that locked door might contain. What would happen if they opened the door and walked into that room? Would they discover something shameful? Would they discover something tragic? Would they discover a piece of themselves that was irredeemable? This "other woman" cannot be hidden away but must be fleshed out as my children grow. They are a piece of her, and she is a piece of them, and it's not tragic or shameful.

I drove from the jail free from the chains I wore when I walked in. Because I know God has forgiven the inexcusable in me, and He does not carry a file filled with all my crimes. He knows I'm not the bad things I've done, just like I'm not the good things I've done either. I'm just a mom trying to love the best I can with the pieces that I have. And this journey of forgiveness is every day. It is me giving up my hope for a better past, and it's harder than I ever imagined.

I guess we aren't so different after all.

> "He knows I'm not the bad things I've done, just like I'm not the good things I've done either. I'm just a mom trying to love the best I can with the pieces that I have."

the Roundtable

with IVAN KEIM, JERRY D. MILLER,
EMILY HERSHBERGER, & DANIEL MILLER

Illustrations by: SETH YODER

Ivan, Emma, and their four children live on a 12-acre homestead where they strive to raise as much of their own food as possible. Each year they have a large garden, harvest from their orchard, use raw milk from their own cow, and process chicken, turkey, beef, and pigs for their freezers. Ivan is a minister in the local Amish community. He builds tiny homes and animal shelters for a living.

Jerry and Gloria Miller, along with their six children, operate Gloria's home farm, a 173-acre organic dairy. They milk between 60 and 70 cows with a few small cottage industries supplementing the farm income. Jerry is a deacon in his local Amish church.

Emily Hershberger, with her husband and two children, have an organic dairy near Mt Hope, Ohio. She enjoys farming, gardening, garage sales, and a good book.

Daniel and Mae live on a 93-acre farm between Walnut Creek and Trail, Ohio. Five children, hay-making, and Black Angus cattle take up any spare time after work at Carlisle Printing.

the Roundtable

AMISH INSIGHTS ON:
TECHNOLOGY

Question:

The balance between the blessings and pit-falls of modern-day technology can be hard to find. How do we balance using technology with staying connected to our community?

Answered by:

Ivan Keim & **Jerry D. Miller**

Originally published in January, 2023

Ivan: "How do we balance using technology with staying connected to our community?" This is a more complex question than can be answered in a short column, but we will focus on a few key areas where technology is challenging us as a society. How do we view technology? What is technology? Webster's Dictionary defines technology as "the totality of the means employed to provide objects necessary for human sustenance and comfort." Imagine the mode of transportation since the beginning of time: humans and animals were designed to walk. If we wanted to move from one location to the next, we moved our legs and walked. Animals were hitched to sleds or other objects as they dragged them over the ground to move them, and then they added wheels to make it easier to pull. They could now carry more weight and pull it greater distances. This increased the comfort level for its users.

For thousands of years, man relied on animal power to pull their wagons with goods and people until the 1800s when the steam engine was attached to this wheel-driven technology that had been developed centuries prior. Technology has continued to improve our mode of transportation over the last 250 years. We can now travel across the globe in less than a day.

When Henry Ford started producing cars for the masses in the 1920s, our Amish forefathers were concerned that it would harm our family unit and be a hindrance to our communities. They

> **"Controlled access to motor vehicles keeps faith with tradition while giving just enough freedom to maneuver in the larger society. It allows the use of modern technology without being enslaved by it or allowing it to fray the social fabric."**

chose to stay with horse and buggy transportation. This has kept us closer together and limits the ability to come and go with ease. As family members moved to other communities and employment started to move away from the farm, it also brought some challenges. Today we have a network of taxi drivers that provide transportation in times of need when horse and buggy does not suffice. We can still see the benefit of horse and buggy travel to keep us together as a community, but we have recognized the need for occasional motor vehicle transportation. In his book *What the Amish Teach Us*, Donald Kraybill states the following:

Controlled access to motor vehicles keeps faith with tradition while giving just enough freedom to

maneuver in the larger society. It allows the use of modern technology without being enslaved by it or allowing it to fray the social fabric.

In this same way, we are being challenged with electronic technology, from the phone to the computer to the internet, which seems to connect everything in today's world. Some churches have opted to say "no" to all means of electronic technology, while others have chosen to use some of it, but with limitations.

Electronic technology is challenging the way that we relate to each other. Deep, meaningful relationships fulfill our lives. When we have conversations with each other, we get to know what the other person is experiencing. If we stop long enough to truly listen and understand what our friend is saying, we can understand how he is feeling. More is said by our body language and tone of voice than the actual words that are said. Electronic communication has advanced so rapidly over the years that it has replaced a lot of our face-to-face communication. Electronic communication cannot replace the emotions and feelings that are shared when we look somebody in the eye and see their excitement or feel their pain.

———————

This fall, our son shot his first deer during the youth gun season. When we came home, we could all partake in the joy as he relayed the experience to his mom and his sisters. There were cheers and excitement and they saw his beaming eyes, complete with all the emotions experienced at a time like this. If we had sent home a quick text message, "kenneth shot deer," the value of sharing the moment and the electricity with sharing it firsthand would have died off by the time we got home.

> **"Electronic communication cannot replace the emotions and feelings that are shared when we look somebody in the eye and see their excitement or feel their pain."**

As our society relies more and more on electronic communication, we lose the ability to have those meaningful relationships that pull us together. We are able to relay messages better and quicker, but is it bringing us closer together?

Ever since the beginning of time when God said, "It is not good that man should be alone,"[1] man has longed to be in relationship with others. When Jesus walked on the Earth, he explained, "Thou shalt love the Lord thy God with all thy heart, and with all thy soul, and with all thy mind. This is the first and great commandment. And the second is like unto it, thou shalt love thy neighbour as thyself."[2] We have been designed with a desire to be part of something that is greater than us. We get a feeling of satisfaction and accomplishment when we belong to a group of people who are working towards a greater cause.

When we belong to something, we also have a responsibility that comes with accountability. Growing up, we all belonged to a family. Each family had their set of rules that we abided by, and if we did not conform, there were consequences.

In the digital world, we can now belong to a "community" that has no responsibilities or accountability. There are online platforms for pretty much any interest that you may have. If it comes to the point where we do not agree, we just drop out. There are no responsibilities, and I am not accountable to anybody. In the end, this "relationship" does not bring the joy and fulfillment that a one-on-one relationship brings. It also does not teach us the grit and hard work that a good relationship requires. We get so used to just "dropping out" if it does not go well that we struggle to learn the art of "getting along with other people."

With general society completely immersed in electronic technology and the Plain communities trying to traverse the raging waters of this digital sea, we are all affected by it. So what can we do to tame the tiger—or at least cage it—so that it will not devour us all?

First, for the people who are used to having electronic communication at their fingertips all the waking hours of the day, there are a few questions to ponder.

Are you willing to lay it aside and enjoy the people around you?

Can you shut off all communication devices during meals and family time?

Would it be possible to eliminate electronic communication outside of work hours?

May I go so far as to suggest removing the TV from the main room of the house? Or consider this: are you willing to remove it altogether?

Start by setting an evening aside each week to do something together as a family with no electronic interruptions. Play a board game. Do a work project together. Take a walk through the woods, and enjoy the natural beauty that God created.

In the last chapter of his book, *Surviving the Tech Tsunami*, Gary Miller shares this with us:

Our churches must be awake, aware, and actively addressing this issue. But we cannot stop there. Not everyone is blessed to be part of a fellowship that is seriously confronting this problem. Therefore, it is essential that we prepare personally for the coming onslaught. Regardless how often your congregation meets (and it should be often), or how much dialogue you have (and there should be plenty), or how much thought you give to collective agreements (and that should be much), ultimately it will be your personal connection with God that will empower you to survive and thrive in this tech tsunami.

If you would like to learn more on the subject of technology, *Surviving the Tech Tsunami* by Gary Miller is a good read.

---

1) Genesis 2:18   2) Matthew 22:37–39

Jerry: Unless the Lord builds the house, those who labor build it in vain.[1] Jesus taught us in the Sermon on the Mount, "Seek ye first the kingdom of God, and all these things shall be added unto you."[2]

So you ask, how do we balance using technology and community? Maybe for starters, we have to recognize that not all technology is wrong. I, for one, am thankful for the technology that brought us toilet paper, as I have no desire to go back to the Sears and Roebuck days. As a person from the Plain community, we have the tendency to view something new as dangerous, and rightly so. Still, the Bible does not necessarily teach that new things are wrong or sinful in themselves, but it says the lust of the flesh—the lust of the eye and the pride of life[3]—is what's sinful. If I continually want my own thing in my own way, I know that leads to death. The Biblical view naturally leads us to a life of counterculture and nonconformity to the old, sick society. We are called to build a culture that heals instead of destroys. This is an exciting process of liberation.

We must realize that righteousness is not isolated (me by myself); that is self-righteousness. As we become righteous, our relationships take on real flesh and blood—our visions, goals, and desires we share with real human beings, not some techno-visual-electrified being without a soul. We must remember the great Achilles' heel of the technosphere in which we live is that it doesn't make us as happy as it claims. Therefore, we must actively seek ways to limit technology and do more ourselves. The old proverb, "If you want a friend, be a friend," still holds true. If we truly desire the comradery of a neighbor, we must be a neighbor; this means eating together, working together, and crying together. These actions build relationships that stand the test of time.

As I consider the moral decay of society and how technology has contributed to it, it behooves me to think about how I grew up and how vastly different it is now. Growing up, I knew instinctively that every man was our neighbor and stood for things rightly. Our neighbors did everything they possibly could to protect us boys from ourselves; we knew that without being told, and it protected us from pornography and all its evil influences.

Now we have fathers willing to give little Johnny a device that connects him directly to the

pits of Hell with the admonition, "Please, Johnny, don't look at it." Who are we kidding?!

Yes, I realize we need a certain amount of tech to survive in the business world. But I also see a good friend of mine who operates a furniture business without a cell phone or email, and he still walks 500 yards to the neighbor to use his telephone. His business is thriving, and he stays busy without this technology. He told me recently,

> "As I consider the moral decay of society and how technology has contributed to it, it behooves me to think about how I grew up and how vastly different it is now."
>
> - Jerry D. Miller

"If I had a phone in my office, I would become a total slave to it." The old tenets of honesty, workmanship, and integrity still hold true. This is especially true because more and more people long to do business with a person, not a machine. As a general rule, the more machines, the less community.

We need to reaffirm the importance of the Sabbath day: times of rest and fasting from production and consumption. Time spent in solitude, resting, and waiting without the interruption of technology. We must view community as essential; in other words, the needs of my neighbor exceed my own. We must approach technology with open skepticism, or we become slaves to our choices. Therefore stand fast in the liberty wherein ye are called.[4] 🐦

1) Psalm 127:1a   2) Matthew 6:33
3) 1 John 2:15–16   4) Galatians 5:1

the Roundtable

AMISH INSIGHTS ON:
FORGIVENESS

Question:

How do you practice forgiveness in your community?

Answered by:

Jerry D. Miller *&* **Ivan Keim**

Originally published in May, 2023

Jerry: In any close-knit community, forgiveness is the elixir that cures disease. It cleans the cancer from the joints and makes things pliable again. The spiritual WD-40 that lessens the creaking and groaning. Forgiveness is counter-cultural. It flies in the face of conventional thinking. Society teaches us that we claim what is ours no matter the cost—we claim our rights. Jesus taught us to turn the other cheek, and not only to turn the other cheek physically but inwardly as well. A heart change that expresses itself in a daily walk with my neighbor.

Maybe one of the most visible displays of forgiveness in recent history was the Nickel Mines incident when a troubled young man entered an Amish schoolhouse and took hostage 10 young innocent school girls, bound them, laid them in a row on the floor, and proceeded to shoot them execution style. Five died and all the others were left to deal with scars—both emotionally and physically—that we can only imagine. The young man then proceeded to kill himself.

The public display of forgiveness went viral—nationally and internationally, people could not understand. How can you extend the olive branch under such circumstances? This bitter young man was known locally in the community—his parents had provided taxi work to some of the victims' families. The response was immediate, showing up at the perpetrator's door, simply embracing the raw emotion by extending an open palm. No hard feelings. We forgive. We'll get through this together. It stunned the watching world.

While we don't believe such a heinous act is the will of God, we do believe God can use such acts to portray goodness through His people. Yes, I know the public display of spontaneous forgiveness was beautiful. I also know the private battle endured as they shed buckets of tears.

The slow process of healing, the hard work of every morning once again renewing the vow to forgive was a long journey. Perhaps one of the first Bible verses most Amish children learn to memorize is the Lord's prayer. *Forgive us our debts as we forgive our debtors.*[1] The reality is, as we are willing to

Painting by Elsie Beiler in 2006 in remembrance of the Nickel Mines shooting.

forgive others, so the Lord forgives us. We are all sinners, and we all fall short of God's grace. We would do well to realize that not only do I have to put up with my neighbors' shortcomings, but really, he has to put up with mine.

The refusal to forgive causes bitterness, it jaundices our view of our fellow man. And so very often, the very things we cannot forgive, we become—because our focus is wrong. Forgiveness not only releases others; it releases us. It is good

"Five trees silently lift their branches skyward, a memorial to what happened. No great fanfare, no big applause. Just five trees commemorating where Nickel Mines Schoolhouse used to stand. A monument of what happened by God's grace—His marvelous gift of forgiveness."

for the immune system: it lowers blood pressure, slows the heart rate, lessens depression, calms anxiety, releases strain on the vocal cords, and strengthens marriages. It is completely opposite of what society teaches us. "To err is human, to forgive is divine," as the saying goes. Vengeance, we believe, is God's work, leaving us with little energy to settle the score ourselves.

In most Plain communities every spring and fall—twice a year—the church gathers for what is called "*Ordnung gma*" or council meeting, a sort of moral housecleaning ceremony where members are reminded of their Christian obligation to be honest and upright; to simply be neighborly, to help where help is needed, to exercise our hearts in the moral responsibility towards our fellow man—and this includes forgiveness. In the Nickel Mines case, no edicts were needed, no appointed ambassadors, just human beings doing the hard work of mending relationships and restoring harmony. Remember, God's grace is sufficient for every situation.

---

1) Matthew 6:12, 15

Ivan: Forgiveness is one of Jesus' key messages that he taught his disciples when he walked on this earth. It is also one of the hardest things for our carnal nature to practice. Jesus' teachings from the Sermon on the Mount included...

And forgive us our debts, as we forgive our debtors. But if ye forgive not men their trespasses, neither will your Father forgive your trespasses.[1]

Many of our ancestors suffered for their faith in Europe before coming to America. Dirk Willems gave us a good example of forgiveness and loving your enemy. In the winter of 1569, in the country of Holland, Dirk Willems was to be apprehended because of his faith. As he was running to escape, he was being chased by a "bounty hunter." Racing out over the wintry countryside, he treacherously made his way over the ice. When Dirk reached the other shore, he heard the cries of his pursuer as he broke through the ice. He could have raced to freedom. He could have made it home to his mother and his sister, but he chose to inch his way out over the ice and pull his pursuer to safety. This act of kindness cost Dirk his life. When he arrived on the shore after his heroic efforts, he was promptly captured by the town burgomaster and was later convicted of heresy because of his faith in Jesus Christ. He was condemned to be burned at the

stake. Dirk chose to turn the other cheek and put the teachings of Jesus into action.

Monumental decisions like this do not happen in the spur of the moment, but rather by a lifetime of smaller decisions that lead up to it. Dirk's decision to risk his own life to save the life of his pursuer was not made at the moment that he stood on the shore, but more so by his conscious effort to live out Jesus' teachings in his daily life. It is easy for us to know what we should do, but it is a lot harder to put it into action.

The following story happened in our community a number of years ago. On a beautiful summer day, with not a cloud in the sky, 15-year-old Jeffrey* leisurely rode his bicycle down the road. At the same time, Mark Stevens* was distracted by something in the car and crossed left of center, hitting Jeffrey head-on. The impact left no hope of survival, and Jeffrey was pronounced dead at the scene. The community and neighborhood fell into shock as they prepared for the funeral. We do not plan for situations like this. How do you respond

"Unwillingness to forgive is like drinking poison and hoping our offender will die from it."

– Ivan Keim

to a situation like this? We can choose to be bitter, or we can choose to forgive. Following is part of a letter by Jeffrey's parents that was read at Mark's sentencing...

"We forgive Mark for the accident. He is very sorry. He is very likable with good manners. We feel very sorry for him."

If we choose to forgive, it releases our pent-up emotion and allows us to begin the healing process from a wrongdoing or an unkind remark about us. It could have been accidental or intentional. In turn, if we hold a grudge, we cannot begin that healing process and will relive the incident, making it harder and harder to heal. Unwillingness to forgive is like drinking poison and hoping our offender will die from it. If we are faced with a decision to forgive or to hold a grudge, let us be reminded of Jesus' words on the cross. *Father, forgive them; for they know not what they do.*[2]

1) Matthew 6:12, 15   2) Luke 23:34

*names changed to protect identity

the Roundtable

AMISH INSIGHTS ON:

FEAR OF OTHERS

Question:

How do you overcome the fear of what other people think?

Answered by:

Emily Hershberger *&* **Daniel Miller**

Originally published in October, 2023

Emily: "Keeping up with the Joneses" is an age-old saying and something many people have tried to attain. Why do we worry about what other people think, and spend so much energy on something that is so unnecessary and, really, rather pointless? Isn't there a smidgen of pride to think we're so important that people will notice if we do or don't measure up. But, in all reality, fretting about what others think of you is something we have all probably dealt with at one point of our lives, especially us women.

Maybe some men worry about this as well, but the men around me sure don't seem to waste too much time stressing about it, so that helps me keep things in perspective. Plus, it seems trying to keep up usually affects your bank account. This reminds me how, recently, David came home from the tack sale in Mt. Hope, pleased with his purchases. As he was telling me about his day, he said he got some really good halters for the mules at $4.25 a piece, which he thought was a tremendous deal. Of course, he said, the Cleveland Browns orange color might have had something to do with the good price, but that's fine with him. I found it amusing but was impressed with his frugality, and as far as the color... shouldn't we all root for the underdog?

It might be harder for us women at times, but who of us doesn't enjoy being with a friend who is totally comfortable with herself and enjoys things in life simply because of who she is, not what she thinks she should be. The friend who has frilly curtains in her kitchen window, not because it's the latest trend, but because she likes how the breeze flutters them on a summer day. She doesn't worry that some people might not consider the décor in her house chic but strives to have a warm and welcoming home. This is the friend who likes you for yourself, and don't we all want to be such a person?

We get the *Smithsonian* magazine, and sometimes there's a short article on fashion, which I find rather fascinating. In our opinion, the ultra-skinny runway models wearing ridiculous looking clothes are very worldly and something far removed from us, but truthfully, aren't we supposed Plain People guilty of having fashion shows ourselves? A new style comes along and we follow, not actually thinking for ourselves. Can't that be worldly as well? Hear me right—I'm talking to myself because anybody who knows me knows I like pretty things, and this can be a battle for me. Here are some things that help me, *IF* I apply them!

When I'm tempted to buy certain clothes, I remind myself that I'm middle aged, have some extra weight, and I'm really going to inspire nobody by trying to follow the trends of teenage girls and young married women. Seriously, who am I kidding! My sister and I would have been horrified and lost respect for Mom if she would have started making her dresses like ours. Why would my daughter think differently?

We are accountable for our children, and it is our responsibility to teach them of God's ways. Both of our children's birthmothers specifically asked us to protect their child from the snares of the world. This looks daunting to me, but as most parents would agree, our children will look to us as examples, so that responsibility should feel weighty. How can we expect our children to handle peer pressure if we ourselves are controlled by it? It is my duty as a mother to try to teach my young daughter the need for modesty, even if it isn't "vogue." I cannot miraculously expect her

> **"Living a life of contentment and knowing that our heavenly Father cares for us is the most powerful tool in overcoming the fear of what other people think."**

to come asking for wider skirts and more pleats once she hits adolescence. It helps me to look at the big picture and think about the future when I'm sewing for my daughter.

Someone once told me that our wants will be our children's needs, and thinking over that has helped me many times when I thought I needed to have this certain thing everybody was raving about. The last thing most of us want is to have our daughters think they need the best of the best once they're married and shovel the money out the back door faster than the young husbands bring it in!

Living a life of contentment and knowing that our heavenly Father cares for us is the most powerful tool in overcoming the fear of what other people think. He created us, and we all have different strengths and weaknesses, so why not embrace that instead of doing the exhausting job of worrying about other people's opinions.

Is there another ditch when it comes to being a free thinker and being comfortable in one's own skin? Just because you personally don't think a standard in church is necessary, does that give you the right to do as you please, only because you don't think you have to be like everybody else? We talked to a minister about this once and his opinion was: It is usually pride or arrogance that brings this thinking, and if you're truly content with who you are, you will not feel the need to try to make a statement, be it liberal or conservative. Hmmmmmm... Something to mull over and ponder.

Life can be messy, and there are no easy answers to some of these questions, but keep in mind—the Joneses really aren't all that great, and you might even find them frightfully dull.

Daniel: To come right down to it, it's not so much about the other people as it is about you. Integrity keeps your priorities in the right place... *"in lowliness of mind let each esteem others better than themselves..."*[1] "Gelassenheit" (yieldingness) and respect; this mutual "esteeming" creates an ideal environment for the fruits of righteousness.[2] Respect—just plain old respect—goes a long way in overcoming the fear of what other people think. Regardless of whether respect is reciprocated or not, in keeping with Mother Teresa's *Do It Anyway* poem, respect the other people anyway.

Saint John writes the fascinating account of Jesus and Nathanael. After Jesus found Philip and told him, follow me, Philip sought his friend Nathanael and said, *"We have found him, of whom Moses in the law, and the prophets, did write, Jesus of Nazareth, the son of Joseph." And Nathanael said unto him* [with a good deal of disrespect], *Can there any good thing come out of Nazareth? Phillip saith unto him, Come and see. Jesus saw Nathanael coming to him, and* [of all things]*saith of him, Behold, an Israelite indeed, in whom is no guile! Nathanael saith unto him, Whence knowest thou me? Jesus answered and said unto him, Before Philip called thee, when thou wast under the fig tree, I saw thee."*[3] It dawned on Nathanael then that Jesus not only saw him under the fig tree but saw into his heart. Jesus knew fully well the remark Nathanael had made, yet extended respect to him, and on top of that, an accolade. Altogether, it made Nathanael change his tune in an awful hurry. *"Rabbi, thou art the Son of God; thou art the King of Israel."*[4]

Never forget: to anyone else you are part and parcel of the other people. Proper respect is in your best interest. In olden times, God displayed little tolerance for unfair criticism, especially against his servant Moses. He dealt harshly with the perpetrators. It's a bit of a paradox, isn't it, that the defining characteristic of the greatest leader in history was this: *"Now the man Moses was very meek, above all men which were on the face of the earth."*[5]

Our focus should be on what is spiritually and morally right, not on what other people think. Consider Martin Luther back in the year 1517, or Martin Luther King, for that matter. Many people in the course of history have risen above popular opinion, taken a stand for what's right and suffered the consequences. Yet right will always prevail, if not in this life, surely in the life to come.

All of us know that... *"perfect love casteth out fear..."*[6] And that takes me down memory lane. Our married daughter Lisa and little granddaughter Michelle came home to spend the day. Lisa lifted Michelle from the buggy, and as soon as her little feet hit the ground, she made a beeline for me. "Dawdy, Dawdy,"* she sang out happily. "Doh bin ich!" (Here I am!) That was an unforgettable moment. The little girlie felt supremely secure in the fact that we thought only the best of her. As a result, she could be herself in a wonderful, unfettered way—no restraint, no fear. It occurred to me then how a lack of true love and respect on our part could restrict and reduce the effectiveness of those around us.

On the lighter side, another key to overcoming the fear of what other people think is birthdays—more birthdays equal more experience, which equals more moxie in coping with life's vicissitudes and divided opinions. Simply doing what is right lends an inner power to take the high road while maintaining an attitude of respect. 🐦

---

1) Philippians 2:3b   2) Galatians 5:22-23   3) John 1:43-48
4) John 1:49   5) Numbers 12:3   6) I John 4:18
*Grandpa

Widows Path

with FERREE HARDY

Ferree Hardy has helped thousands of widows through her book, *Postcards from the Widows' Path*, small groups, speaking, and personal coaching, but touching one life at a time is what matters most to her. She holds a BA from Moody Bible Institute and was a pastor's wife in Ohio for over twenty years before her first husband died. She's happily remarried now, living in Ticonderoga, NY, and her readers know that moving seems to have become a hobby for her. But she also enjoys backyard chickens, aims to read fifty books a year, and loves to bake.

Words by: Ferree Hardy

Originally published in March, 2022

The Ministry of Presence

I SUSPECTED my friend was having a hard time, but I didn't know for certain until another friend phoned me; she told me to go to our friend's house and let myself in. When I got there, I knocked on the door and cautiously opened it. There she was, sitting on the floor of the kitchen, rocking back and forth. The friend who'd called sat next to her. At first, I was confused. Did we need to go to the emergency room, I wondered? But it didn't make any sense: they were both crying. I hurried over and sat down on the floor. When I heard the news, I cried too.

"Ministry of presence" is a term used by chaplains and grief counselors for a very effective way that friends and family can help grieving people—just be there. At the time, I didn't know it was "a ministry"

> **"...you don't need to bear the responsibility for saying anything. You understand that you cannot fix suffering people with your words."**

to sit on the kitchen floor and cry with my friends, but it was. I probably should have stayed longer.

Do you remember the story of Job? His three friends illustrate the ministry of presence. *"Now when Job's three friends heard of all this evil that was come upon him, they came every one from his own place... for they had made an appointment together to come to mourn with him and to comfort him. And when they lifted up their eyes afar off, and knew him not, they lifted up their voice, and wept; and they rent every one his mantle, and sprinkled dust upon their heads toward heaven. So they sat down with him upon the ground seven days and seven nights, and none spake a word unto him: for they saw that his grief was very great."* (Job 2:11-13 KJV)

This is a perfect example of the ministry of presence. They wept with Job. Romans 12:15 commands us to *"weep with those who weep."* Job's friends did well at first, but then—unfortunately—they opened their mouths. Pent-up questions, arguments, and accusations boiled over, growing worse and worse until God Himself stepped in. To be fair to Job's friends, I think we'd all agree it'd be hard to sit with someone for seven days without saying a word. Maybe that's why it's considered a ministry. It's not always easy, and it takes patience and self-control.

The most important thing to know about the ministry of presence is that you don't need to bear the responsibility for saying anything. You understand that you cannot fix suffering people

with your words. There's no recipe for grieving—a little bit of this, a little bit of that; stir; let it simmer for an hour, and then you can move on—No! Instead, you come alongside and feel the burden of pain that weighs on your friend. You realize that you don't have the power to lift that burden, but you do have the ability to silently pray, listen, and lift the grief to the God who does have the power to lift up the downcast soul.

Funerals are a public opportunity for the ministry of presence. You might think no one will notice if you do not attend, but what if no one else came either? Your simple presence is greatly appreciated. Cards, meals, and visits afterwards are too, even if they are months later. It's better to receive late condolences than none at all.

The ministry of presence means that you reach out to the widow and widower. You go to visit them. This doesn't have to take all day. You also include them in your life. Sit with them in church. Church is often the loneliest spot on the planet for widows and widowers. Invite them to

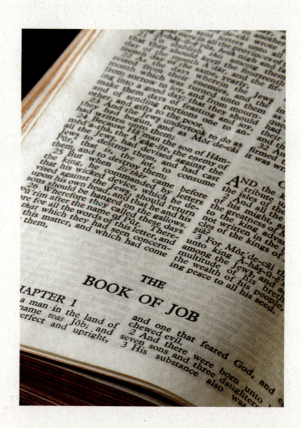

your gatherings, even when you think they will say no. Please keep asking and inviting; it shows that you care.

If you've not been widowed, you probably don't understand why it's so hard for some people to adjust to widowhood. But after the death of a spouse, everything drastically changes.

Try to imagine walking into your own house the day after the funeral. It's so quiet and empty that your footsteps almost echo. Your heart pounds; you hear each breath you take. Or you might unconsciously hold your breath and feel like you're suffocating. You don't hear your spouse's familiar greeting when you come home. Your bed is empty, and the sheets are cold. You might not have anyone to eat supper with. Or, if you're a parent with children at home, there's no one who can give you a break when you have a splitting headache or the flu. This is why a ministry of presence is so important; the loss is so huge. It's unspeakable—there are no words to describe the depth. Mere words cannot fix it.

The PRESENCE of people is what matters. This means you don't tell a widow, "Let me know if you need anything." That's too vague, and it's too much of a job for her. She won't let you know. She can't! Her life is in chaos and shock; she has no idea what she needs.

Instead, offer her your presence and your ordinary friendship. "Ordinary" and "normal" are precious commodities when life seems to have shattered. Small talk about the weather and the neighborhood is fine because it's familiar. Also share your favorite memories, but be sensitive so that it's not all about you and your experiences. Don't compare others' losses either. Make it a two-way conversation so the widower can open up and talk if he or she would like. Ask questions, listen well, sit, and chat.

The ministry of presence takes time. I'm often in too much of a rush, but I'm learning and growing.

Will you learn with me? It all starts with a compassionate heart and being a good friend. Do like Job's friends did at first: "*...No one said a word to him because they saw how great his suffering was.*" Just be there. 🕊

Until next month,

ferree ♥

Words by: Ferree Hardy

Originally published in June, 2023

When a Phone Call Marks the Darkest Night

IT MIGHT BE FROM A DOCTOR'S OFFICE, the police, or even a relative or friend, but it's a parent's worst nightmare—to pick up the phone and hear words that fracture their existence—"Your child is gone." It doesn't happen to everyone, but no one is exempt.

A retired pastor and his wife graciously shared their experience with me while they were packing for a flight to Alaska in January. I hope the warmth of a June day will soften this cold reality of grief.

What Happened?

Marlin and Sharon Beachy, having moved from Alaska to Ohio only the year before, bolted awake when their phone rang at 3:09 a.m. on the day after Father's Day, 2013. Sharon's brother, Dan, was calling from Alaska. "I've got some bad news," he said to prepare them. Their son Ryan, 29, had just been killed; his motorcycle had hit a moose. Topping almost 1,600 pounds, a full-grown moose is the largest animal in Alaska.

Stunned, they had to ask and know for sure if Dan had said, "Ryan," their son, or "Brian," Sharon's other brother. Dan confirmed he'd said "Ryan." After they hung up the phone, Marlin called Dan back. "I had to call him back. I couldn't believe it." Then the state troopers called to confirm the report.

Only an hour earlier, the sun hadn't yet set in that part of "The Land of the Midnight Sun." As Ryan motorcycled up a hill, it glared directly into his eyes. Visibility was also cut by a smoky haze from distant wildfires, and then that moose ambled onto the road. State troopers found no skid marks. Ryan was killed instantly, and so was the moose. Ryan's girlfriend was thrown from the motorcycle; she survived, although with serious injuries.

"For months following, I'd wake up at 3:00 in the morning," said Marlin. "I'd look at the clock. And then, I'd tell myself, "Oh, at least it's not 3:09." Such happenings are the mechanics of grief.

Within hours, Marlin and Sharon had boarded a flight to Anchorage, Alaska.

Sharon said, "We worked through every parent's nightmare over the next few days: writing your child's obituary, planning a funeral service..." Ryan's memorial service would be held at Glacierview Bible Church, where Marlin had pastored for 25 years before being called to another ministry.

Was Anyone Able to Help Them?

Although Marlin and Sharon had moved back to Ohio, Glacierview Bible Church was still without a pastor. Who would shepherd Ryan's family through the valley of the shadow of his death? As it turned out, a retired pastor was nearby, on staff at a Bible camp. Coincidentally, his son had died in an accident years before. Another nearby pastor had also experienced the loss of a child.

These two pastors, acquainted with grief, stepped in to minister. "This isn't just Marlin and Sharon," the Beachys realized. "Many others have also lost a child."

"We found out right away that people who'd walked through this were really helpful. They didn't have to say a thing. They just knew."

"The most helpful thing people did was to simply come, sit quietly, and cry with us. A lot of chatter didn't help at all. Your brain can only handle so much at that point," Marlin and Sharon agreed.

Sharon also went on to explain, "The church totally took care of us. I didn't have to cook. They brought meals. Someone cleaned my house. We still owned our old house in Alaska, and Ryan had been using it, but only between jobs—a couple of days a month. He had an average guy's housekeeping skills, so this was a big help!"

Marlin reminisced, "I just remember that you're in your own little world. You can't believe it happened. Shock—the emotional shock—protects you from the pain. For me, it was maybe six months before the shock wore off. Then the pain set in and all the questions came."

What Did This Do to Their Faith?

Eventually, both Sharon and Marlin asked, "Do we really believe what we believe?"

"We really had to wrestle with that," said Sharon.

Marlin added, "All these years I'd been telling people, 'God's in control. He's ordained. He's allowed. He works for our good and His glory...' It's all fine and good to say that. But when you experience this kind of pain, the question is—do you really believe?"

"We kept saying, 'It's not supposed to be like this.' Then an associate pastor asked us, 'Where does it say that in the Bible?' He said it gently, but he was right."

"You've got to have that foundation, that bedrock of faith foundation. Believe in God's goodness and sovereignty before those hard things come," said Marlin.

"We really felt that God was walking with us through this. It doesn't relieve the pain, but the knowledge He is there... It was like His hand was reaching down and He was holding on to me," said Sharon. "To turn away from God would be to turn to despair. We couldn't do that," she added.

"It's a long process," they both agreed, "but the turning point in pain was coming to peace with the fact that God allowed it."

How Did This Affect Their Marriage?

Sharon admitted, "One of the things I struggled with was that I wasn't as emotional as Marlin. I'm the mother! I should be bawling my eyes out! I questioned, 'What kind of mom am I?'"

Marlin said, "I shed tears probably every day for a year."

"I didn't," said Sharon, "and that was hard for me."

Instead, Sharon read a lot. *Lament for a Son* by Nicholas Wolterstorff, and *Holding on to Hope* by Nancy Guthrie, were very powerful helps.

"It's like we were on parallel train tracks. We cried together, we prayed together. But we were also in our own world of grief. It didn't tear us apart, but we needed other people for help. We needed to allow each other to grieve in their own way, and not be critical."

How Has Life Changed for Them?

"This opened our eyes to how often this happens. You're not aware of it until it happens to you. We're far more compassionate now," they agreed.

Marlin shared, "It made me more intentional to connect with our daughters, Melissa and Rachel. We're not guaranteed another moment in this life. I am now inclined to do things that don't make a lot of sense, just to spend time with our girls and grandkids. For example, last fall I went to Alaska for our grandson's birthday! And I've become more intentional with calling."

Sharon added, "We've never been party people, but now, not at all. We're more serious. We're not killjoys—we can still be pretty goofy. Yet, here we are, ten years later, and we still miss Ryan something fierce. The difference is that we can talk about him now. We LIKE to talk about him. We are joyous."

Key Points for Those Who Haven't Gone Through This Kind of Loss:

"**First, cultivate a deep relationship with the Lord** because these things will happen. Maybe not the loss of a child, but life is hard. You've got to be walking with the Lord, and be in a good community."

"**Don't live in fear.** Entrust your children to the Lord. We dedicated Ryan to the Lord when he was a baby. He was God's child, not ours, forever."

"**Don't grieve before your time.** Honor life by loving your children to the fullest. Do crazy things in order to see them. Do like we do—go to Alaska for a weekend, or go in the middle of winter!"

"**Don't dwell on death.** It's not healthy and it's not helpful. If God deems it His will to call them home, He'll give you the grace you need."

"Pain is the price of love. If we didn't love Ryan, we wouldn't miss him," Sharon said.

"It's been an amazing journey," said Marlin. "We didn't know it, but God was preparing things. Ryan was calling us more often. His friends said he was having more spiritual conversations with them."

Ryan had sent a text to Marlin the day before which read, "Happy Father's Day, Pops." And although there was that most awful phone call in the night, there had also been a wonderful, unexpected call from Ryan just that morning. "I got to talk to him that day!" Marlin fondly exclaimed.

Not a day passes that those of us who've suffered the loss of a loved one don't live with the bittersweet truth that life is precious; our days are numbered. Dear Reader, is there someone with whom you need to talk? Don't wait until it's too late. Be intentional and reach out to them today.

Marlin and Sharon, thank you for touching our lives with Ryan's. 🐦

Until next month,

ferree ♥

Marlin Beachy with his son, Ryan, in Alaska (1988)

Words by: Ferree Hardy
Originally published in September, 2023

Echoes of Loneliness

AS A LITTLE GIRL growing up in the rolling countryside of Wisconsin, I often played outside after supper in the waning days of summertime. Just before sunset, as the air cooled, my younger brothers and I would face the hill up the road and start calling, "Hello! Hello!" A faint "Hello!" would echo back. When school started, we'd sing a song about echoes during music class—"Little Sir Echo." I'll never forget the last line: "...but you're always so far away... away." It was really a song about loneliness; wistful and poignant, it covered a deep ache with the innocence of childhood.

For all who mourn, grief is an ongoing jumble of loneliness and longing, an echo in our heart that says "you're always so far away..." But for widows, widowers, orphans, and parents with empty arms, the loss is a rending of life's strongest human connections: marriage, child and parent, mother and child, father and child. There's an undeniable level of connection when we've bonded through marriage, birth, or adoption. Our loved one has slipped beyond the horizon, like a ship heading out to sea, getting smaller and smaller until it vanishes. Out of sight, but never out of mind.

The Lord understands this loneliness better than a builder understands the strengths and weaknesses of his construction, a farmer the fertility of his fields, or the quilter her designs and color combinations. God knows how loneliness echoes inside our hollow chest. He's our builder, our farmer, and the one who sews our life together. He's our creator; He knows us better than we know ourselves. Nothing takes Him by surprise; no detail is overlooked. Everything matters.

As proof to our doubting hearts, God sent his Son, Jesus Christ, to experience humanity and loneliness. During His forty days of temptation in the wilderness, the silence was interrupted only by a whisper of hot breeze, the skittering of lizard claws across rocks, the cries of birds above, and the oily voice of Satan. A year or two later, Christ prayed alone in the garden of Gethsemane. His disciples fell asleep as He prayed in anguish, with sweat like drops of blood. When Judas arrived with the ultimate betrayal, the disciples woke up and "forsook Him and fled."

Yes, Jesus Christ knows our deepest loneliness. He lived with the tension of separation from his Father, the weaknesses of friends and family, the instability of homelessness, and the torture of temptation.

Therefore, He is patient with us. He will listen to our prayers and pain. When we have no words that can fit, contain, or capture what we

> **"Tell God the truth. And remember this truth: God is not an echo; He understands, and He is with you."**

long to say, He even gives us words to echo. We can use the Lord's Prayer, or others found in the Bible, prayer books, poems, and devotionals. The Bible says "Pray without ceasing," and we really can. Loneliness is pervasive, and prayers can be too. Once we start looking for them. I daresay we might even find a prayer on a poster or a bumper sticker.

Here's a short, honest prayer about loneliness that I've shared with widows. It's like many of the psalms, and even includes a part of Psalm 102 which describes loneliness so well. Does it capture your thoughts too? If so, pray it frequently and unashamedly. God never tires of hearing from you.

Dear Heavenly Father,

There are days when I feel suffocated and overwhelmed by loneliness. It's like a heavy, dark blanket pressing on my face. It drains my strength and hope. Like arthritis, it just won't go away. How can I live like this? How can I go on without the one person I can't live without? The one who was a part of me; who completed my sentences, filled my thoughts, and gave purpose to my days? There is no "me" without them.

"I am like a desert owl, like an owl among the ruins. I lie awake; I have become like a bird alone on a roof." (Psalm 102:6,7)

Please, God, help me. Amen.

Have you been in such a lonely place? Like that bird on the rooftop, watching life pass you by? Sometimes the loneliest place in the world is when we're in a crowd of people, surrounded by so many, but not connected—not belonging.

Prayers of desperation and despair are called "laments." They're expressions of deep sorrow. They provide hope, but they don't tell us why. But really, is there any reason our loved one died that we would be ready to accept? Someday we'll be ready, and ultimately God himself will wipe away every tear. But not today. For now, it's simply best to be honest; cry out to God.

Tell God the truth.

And remember this truth: God is not an echo; He understands, and He is with you.

God is OK with honesty and laments. He wants us to bring the loneliness, pain, and even anger to Him. "Cast all your cares upon Him, for He cares for you." (1 Peter 5:7). Jennifer Sands, a young 9/11 widow, realized that she was angry at God. Then she realized she couldn't be angry at someone who didn't exist. And if He did exist, she must trust Him for her salvation, which she eventually did. If you're lonely today, pray. Ask for help, solace, and salvation.

Lean in and learn about loneliness, lament, and grief. Others have gone through this and hold out their hands to help you through it. Their books are like good friends. Here are some to start with. Ask to borrow them from your local library through inter-library loan; order online or through your local bookstore.

- *A Tempered Faith: Rediscovering Hope in the Ashes of Loss* by Jennifer Sands
- *Hope When Your Heart Is Breaking* by widower, Ron Hutchcraft
- *God's Healing for Life's Losses* by Robert W. Kellemen, PH.D *(chapter three especially focuses on lament)*
- *Dark Clouds Deep Mercy—Discovering the Grace of Lament* by Mark Vroegop

Learn to defeat the discouragement of loneliness by requesting my free *Defeating Discouragement Diary*. Its four pages cover one week, and you may make as many copies as you like. Directions are also included. Email me at hardyferree@gmail.com for a PDF. Echoes of loneliness are echoes of eternity. They stir our soul and remind us that our loved one is "far away...

away." Yet, safe in the arms of Jesus, that man, woman, or child is not alone. And in Christ, in our church, among our dearest friends and family, we are not alone either. Before sunset nears, keep calling, "Hello, hello..."

Until next month,

ferree

Honest
Conversations

with WENDY CUNNINGHAM

Wendy Cunningham is wife to Tom and home-school mom to three amazing gifts from God. In addition to that calling, she is an entrepreneur and author. Her book, *What If You're Wrong?*, blog, and devotionals can be found at gainingmyperspective.com. She is also host of the podcast Gaining My Perspective. Wendy loves Jesus and inspiring people to step into their calling—whatever that might look like in this season. When she's not working, writing, traveling, or podcasting, she can be found homesteading and chasing kids and cows on her farm in Middle Tennessee.

Words by: Wendy Cunningham
Originally published in November, 2022

WHAT IF YOU'RE WRONG?

WHAT AN AMAZING WORK OF GOD that you're reading these words right now. There is so much I want to share with you in the coming months, but I figure the most important thing you need to know about me as we get started is: I'm rescued. Many times over.

It is said God doesn't call the equipped, He equips the called. That's truer in my case than I can tell you. I didn't expect to be a writer or a homesteader—I studied theater! (If you could sneak a peek at my shoe collection, you'd know I *certainly* didn't intend to live on a farm with manure and cows, but God had a plan for that, too.)

Today, I'm grateful for the plot twists He throws my way. And here's the biggest twist: in my early years, I never desired to know God. I was an atheist. But as Philippians 1:6 says, "I am sure of this, that he who started a good work in you will carry it on to completion until the day of Christ Jesus."

God initiated my journey, and He sustains it. And I know now He is faithful to do the heavy lifting all the way to the end. But that doesn't mean we don't have a part to play in this adventure called life. The most challenging and impactful years of my life—coming to know my Father in Heaven—started with a simple question that humbled me: *What if you're wrong?*

This is the question Tom (now my husband) posed when he discovered I didn't believe in God. Not one part of me is left untouched on the other side of those four words. Yes, I was an atheist. So, not only did I not believe in God, I was convinced there couldn't be a God. Even though Tom was anchored in his faith and confident in the truth, mine was not a simple conversion.

> "The most challenging and impactful years of my life started with a simple question that humbled me: *What if you're wrong?*"

When Tom and I started dating in our early twenties, I was terribly lost. The Bible calls it rebellion, and although that's not untrue, *mistaken* is the word I'd choose. After all, I didn't mean to be wrong. Who does?

Imagine growing up in a family that so completely believed in one school of thought that it would never have occurred to you that this school of thought could be incorrect. Generations of my family had rejected God—this was not new. It had always been that way. Growing up in the California public school system, it was not only easy for me to miss God entirely, but I was also given plenty of reasons to believe humans wouldn't need such an entity. It all started with a Big Bang, we evolved from goo, and if you make enough money, there is no need to pray for anything. Trust the science.

My parents and grandparents had built their lives on the premise there was no God, my teachers confirmed that assumption, and my peers challenged none of these things—how was I to know we were all misled? Why would I even suspect?

Now imagine someone coming along, challenging everything you think you know for sure. They ask questions you've not thought of, push buttons that elicit insecurity, and make points that make you wonder—what if I'm wrong?

Obviously, you grow agitated, alarmed, and get defensive. What other reaction would you have? And that's exactly what I did. For years. This is where the enemy lies in wait, folks. He convinces us of falsehoods and sends our ego in to fight to the death. In my case, pride came hard and fast. I was angry. I was frustrated and annoyed with

Wendy, her husband, Tom, and their three children

> **"Growing up in the California public school system, it was not only easy for me to miss God entirely, but I was also given plenty of reasons to believe humans wouldn't need such an entity."**

my new husband. And I was undoubtedly caught off-guard. But there was more at play than just a bruised ego.

I didn't have a plumb line that anchored me and kept me focused on the straight and narrow. Just like when a contractor builds a house, he must first find perfectly level ground. If he starts building on what he assumes is a firm foundation, he'll be long into the process and out a lot of money when he discovers he's built a crooked house. I quickly realized I had built my life on flawed human wisdom, but that was the least of my concerns.

Because I had built my life on shaky ground, there were no guiding principles or values to light my path. As I mentioned, I grew up in the theater. Rejection was my job, flirtation and seduction were my love languages. My value was assigned by whomever was in the position to choose me. Over the years, as you can imagine, those sorts of soul-deep injuries started to fester in my life. Tom found himself on the receiving end of a constant stream of anxiety attacks, bouts of depression, accusations, and issues. Poor guy.

With father figures who were absent or had drug issues and a string of abusive relationships to measure "love" against, trusting others was an up-hill battle for me. Not just trust in Tom, but trust in everything. Not the least of which was a "perfect father" who had allowed me to wander through hell. If God was real, I wasn't convinced I wanted to know any more about Him.

Needless to say, even with God on His side, Tom's work of ministering to me required a tremendous amount of patience. There wasn't a Bible verse to reference, or a quick church invite to throw out that would undo all that had been cemented into place in my life. There may have been a short list of people I trusted, but each and every name on that list believed along with me that a man in the clouds could not be real. Tom was sweet, and maybe there was hope for me beyond all my brokenness, but he was wrong about God. And I could tell it would be a problem in our relationship.

So, I did what anyone else would do when they're certain they're right about something. I set out to prove it. And herein lies the key, the thing that unlocked my salvation and brought a tremendous amount of hope to my husband, the man who was praying for my eternity:

I desired to know what was true more than I wanted to be right.

The irony is, the only reason I set out to find the truth was because I thought I already knew it. But here is the pesky thing about truth: there is only one. Don't let the world tell you otherwise. Absolute truth is just that—absolute. It's not subjective or relative—it doesn't change. By the same measure, God is either real or He isn't; His Word is either sound or not.

Tom knew if I was seeking answers to these questions about God, I'd arrive in the right place. And, like it or not, I was on my way toward that end.

By the grace of God, He saw fit to pluck me right out of all the mess that comes with a lifetime of rejecting His way, and He started to heal my broken heart even before I'd acknowledged His existence. And God began to reveal truth. Not because I deserved it, but because He desired to do it. God knew what Tom knew: what had happened to me was not who I was, and it would not define who I would become. 🐦

~ until next time, Wendy

Words by: Wendy Cunningham
Originally published in July, 2023

SET APART

WE'RE RUINING EVERYTHING. Humans. Have you noticed?

When thinking of farming, you might picture thousands of acres, crop dusters, and giant green tractors. Maybe you conjure up images of a perfectly Pinterest-ed red barn with a white X on well-greased rolling barn doors. Perhaps we have forgotten that until recently—in the grand scheme of humanity—farms were intimate family affairs. Men didn't leave for work in the morning. Well, they didn't leave the farm anyway. Food was grown, harvested, and shared locally. The burden was heavy, but the gratification was high. Oh, and I'm certain the barns were rugged and well-used, but not pretty.

What about school? When you think of school, you might imagine yellow buses, lines of kids following teachers like ducklings, or hundreds of yelling students crammed around lunch tables. But the public school system is a new phenomenon. It's one gigantic experiment. One that's failing to provide the promised value if you ask me. A one-room schoolhouse with multiple grades mixed together—older students teaching younger students—and a teacher selected by the community is more familiar to generations before us. That, or perhaps homeschool—learning from mom around the chores of a busy life on a homestead.

How about church? When I hear that word, huge, blocky buildings come to mind—buildings that look nothing like the steepled architectural specimens of European postcards. I fear it's become more about the coffee bar in the lobby and less about the Holy Spirit in the congregation. Many of us have fallen into the routine of three songs, announcements, message, lunch. Repeat. In so many cases, church has become sterile, void of life. Another box to check.

My husband is a real estate agent, and we've become aware of a movement happening in this country. People are going "back to the land." They're coming from all over the country—mainly they're fleeing coastal cities and states that shall not be named—and they're flooding into places like Texas and Tennessee where we live. I can't tell you how many couples I've met here in the last two years have moved to Middle Tennessee for no other reason than God told them to. We jokingly say that we're here for "the thing" God is going to do.

And yet, as we become aware of the potential errors of modernized civilization—thousand-acre farms in place of homesteads, public school in

> "In so many cases, church has become sterile, void of life. Another box to check."

> ## "We moved to a homestead to become more self-sustaining and to be reminded of where food comes from, to be reconnected to the sacrifices involved."

exchange for homeschool, and giant religious organizations as opposed to community churches—we are trying to restore some of what God might have always intended for His people. I, for one, have been intentionally choosing to go "backward." We moved to a homestead to become more self-sustaining and to be reminded of where food comes from, to be reconnected to the sacrifices involved. After one year in public school, we opted to follow God's prompting and now homeschool our children. And in place of a cookie-cutter (read comfortable and familiar) church, we sought out a spirit-filled, alive congregation with challenging truth coming from the pulpit. And although I knew I was closer to what God had for our family, I still felt something was missing.

These pursuits can be very isolating. And I, an introvert, had fallen into the trap.

In both the modern way of doing things as well as the "new old way," we've forgotten the most important ingredient God always intended to be included...

Community.

My husband used to work for a farmer. He drove a tractor across long expanses of row crops for twelve hours a day. I'm not kidding when I say he would set an alarm on his phone to wake him up when he was about to reach the edge of the field to turn the tractor around. He would spend an entire day alone, never seeing another person. The farmer (not always the owner of the land) took out a huge loan each year, and it was on him to bring the harvest—financial and otherwise. The work, the

risk, and the reward were not shared. Even when another farmer was doing the exact same thing a few miles down the road.

When we're in school, our test results, our grades, and our essays are our own. Everyone hates group projects because we either don't know how to delegate, or we feel most comfortable getting things done ourselves. It never fails that one person in a group will carry an unequal amount of the assignment. We haven't learned the value of shared work and shared accomplishment. It's not taught. Sharing answers is cheating.

And of course, church; just because we may sit in a room full of people does not automatically mean we're in a community. I fully understand and appreciate the appeal of an overly large congregation. There is a peace to slipping into the back row a few minutes late and not feeling pressured to socialize after the fact. And who will really miss us if we don't come at all, right?

God created us to need each other.

When I started to homestead, the first thing I did was find the people in my area who were doing it too. As a matter of fact, after a recent homesteading conference, a few lady friends and I have formed a group where our families will pick one day a month to collectively visit each other's homesteads to work on a bigger project. We all need help sometimes, but how often do we ask? What I've learned the hard way is there are just not enough hands on the farm or hours in the day to accomplish all that needs to be done. I joke with my friends that when you get married you have a bridal shower, when you have a baby there is a baby shower, and when you move to a homestead, there should be a farm shower. I'm coming to understand why people had more children in the past, and why multi-generational living is a critical part of life in most countries.

People need people.

In our case, we've even gone so far as to recruit dear friends to possibly buy some of our land and build on it so we might work together toward a shared vision. Why would we have separate gardens, meat herds, dairy cows, and egg layers when we could share the yoke and benefit of a collective result? Many hands make light work. And the same is true in most circumstances.

I thank God every day for my friend Ashley who became my homeschool mom mentor as I began the journey. She didn't mean to be. She surely didn't volunteer for the role, but she and her kids became my people in a season when I desperately needed support. And even now, I know my kids can easily become isolated in the workload of a farm and the schedule (or lack) of a homeschooler. We need co-ops, sports, friends, and playdates. I have formed a field trip group that meets twice a month. We learn, play, and grow together. It's an important part of development—learning how to be in community, learning how to solve conflict.

At our church, although we have two campuses, and there are thousands of people who attend over many services, we understand the value of intimate community groups. Twice a month we get together with a small number of families, and we break bread, catch up, and "do life together" in a real way. We pray together. And I mean we share vulnerably, cry, and lay hands on one another, firmly believing for miracles to manifest among us.

Community doesn't happen by accident. These endeavors can be godly, but the devil aims high. He has his eye on this movement, these people that are uprooting their lives, breaking free of traditional

"norms," and becoming more independent. We have got to be intentional about staying connected.

Satan wants the focus to be on the independence. And it can easily become an idol.

Vulnerability is never easy, but it is required to establish community. Community can be messy, but it's necessary to steward and share God's gifts and blessings well. I do believe God is calling His people to an old way. We're not supposed to do things the world's way. We can see it's broken—more and more every day—but we're not meant to be separated from each other.

It's when we unite that we can truly be set apart. 🕊

~ until next time, Wendy

> "These endeavors can be godly, but the devil aims high. He has his eye on this movement, these people that are uprooting their lives ... and becoming more independent. We have got to be intentional about staying connected."

Words by: Wendy Cunningham
Originally published in March, 2023

GOD GAPS

WHAT IS FAITH? Hebrews 11:1 tells us, "Now faith is the reality of what is hoped for, the proof of what is not seen." I love that: the proof of what is not seen. Grammatically speaking, faith is a noun. But is that all it is? A "place-holder" reality while we wait for God to fill in the missing pieces? If that's the case, how do we grow in faith?

Faith, like love, is a noun, yes. But it's also a verb—an action word. As Bob Goff's book title *Love Does* suggests, love is an action. It's the practice of loving that exemplifies it. How do you know you're loved? You feel it. Love is an experience.

Faith is the same. How do you know you have faith? You prove it in everything you do (or don't do).

I have learned this lesson many times throughout my walk with God. One such example is my journey from suburbia in Nevada to homesteading in Middle Tennessee. One does not make such a leap without faith. And I believe one most certainly can't walk that road without God.

In 2015, my husband and I sold our home in Nevada and moved into a rental nearby. We believed that God was calling us away from that place, but He hadn't yet revealed where our Promised Land would be. We took several trips up the West Coast, hoping to find our piece of heaven, but nothing felt right.

Well, wouldn't you know it, God chose to reveal our Promised Land at the worst financial moment. It was right there on *Realtor.com* as if it had been cut out of our very dreams and put on the world wide web. The perfect farm. In Tennessee. But a brief phone call to the agent connected to the property revealed that our hope of buying this property was unlikely. It fit our hearts, but it didn't work out in dollars and cents.

It was hard to make sense of what God was doing in that season. I believed He was revealing something. But what? I finally tucked away the experience as a confirmation that what we were hoping for did, in fact, exist. And it existed in Tennessee. That's where we were being called. But the timing was off.

A year (and a lot of distractions) later, we were ready to take out a loan, but the clarity that came in the previous season about Tennessee had fogged over. Was that really where we were being called? Should we go back

> "How do you know you have faith? You prove it in everything you do (or don't do)."

to the drawing board? Our hearts were obedient, but our vision was cloudy.

I don't know about you, but when I need to hear from God, I take a shower. Maybe it's the steam, or perhaps it's the escape from kids for four minutes, but that's where I hear from my Father in Heaven most clearly. One evening in early October of 2016, I found myself in one such prayer session. I asked God for direction and a sign. When I went downstairs, Tom casually informed me that while I was in the shower, the realtor from the Tennessee property we were interested in a year ago had called him—out of the clear blue sky. The farm was still available, and the family wondered if we were still interested.

After the shock of such a specific and quick answer to prayer wore off, I told my husband we had to get on a plane as soon as possible. He believed I was getting ahead of myself, but I believed God was moving, and we needed to respond in faith. Not two weeks later, Tom and I were on a plane to see if Tennessee was going to be our new home.

Faith is a verb.

The memory of that trip is a blur, but I recall one important thing: when I pulled through the tree tunnel that opened up onto the property we now call ours, I knew without a doubt God was saying, "Yes." Nothing else really mattered. I was certain He was going to move mountains. And He'd better because there were quite a few blocking our path forward. I lovingly deemed these obstacles "God gaps." The issues that plagued Tom—like how we'd pay for the farm, where the down payment would come from, the complications of our business and how we'd qualify for a loan—were all just details yet to be worked out. They didn't bother me in the slightest. I had faith, and my faith meant it was assured.

"The reality of things hoped for, the *proof* of what is not seen." My faith was the proof. My husband wasn't convinced.

What transpired over the following months was one of the great miracles of my life. I came to understand what faith in action looks and feels like. And what's more, I had the strange perspective of walking my faith out alongside my husband whose faith told him such an impossible feat could only be achieved in his—my husband's—own strength.

Tom's faith was just a noun. An inanimate object.

By a great miracle and through the accomplishment of a great many phone calls, we qualified for a loan. The first God gap had been closed and we were on our way. I won't say it was smooth sailing, but come January 2017, we were a week from closing on our dream homestead. We

The Tennessee property

> "Faith requires sacrifice. We must give over the glory, but it's an exchange; we don't have to carry the weight. James, Peter, and others tell us to consider it pure joy when we face trials in this life. Trials force us to put our faith into action. And faith is the revelation of a relationship with a good God."

happened to be in Maui with my company when we received a call from our lender. Due to several nuances that were outside of anyone's control and (apparently) foresight, our loan was falling through. Unless we had another $25,000 (and we didn't), it wasn't going to happen.

I saw another God gap that He was going to close for us. Tom saw only defeat.

We flew home from Hawaii determined to figure out our next step. My husband is a fantastic man of God, but this shook him like nothing I've ever seen. I could sense the physical weight on his shoulders, the burden he was carrying, as he tried to close this gap on his own. Strangely, the more I told him God was going to move in our circumstances, the more irritated Tom became.

My faith bothered him.

As the next several hours and days ticked by—the end of the line as it would seem in the natural—my faith only grew stronger while the little my husband held onto crumbled away. So, what is a devoted wife and follower of Christ to do?

I took a shower.

It was a Sunday afternoon—the Sunday before our final day to "save the deal"—and I prayed. I told God I knew He was moving. I believed this was going to work out. I had no fear. But even still, I asked for the solution. What were we supposed to do? Secondly, I reminded God that we were out of time and that we needed guidance that very day. Lastly, and most importantly, I asked God if He would be so generous to give the answer—whatever that answer was—to my husband.

I already had faith. Tom needed the blessing of revelation.

It might be hard to believe, as I'd be tempted to wonder if I hadn't been there myself, but God delivered the most beautiful miracle no more than an hour later. Tom received a phone call from his dad. As God (not luck) would have it, the day our loan fell through, my father-in-law received a piece of mail. That letter was from a former employer—one he worked for nearly two decades before—and it was sent to inform my father-in-law that he had a benefit they were hoping he'd agree to liquidate. Given the fact that he'd take a tax hit to liquidate it, they'd inflated the benefit to $250,000. A multiple of what we needed. My father-in-law was just calling to see if he could offer us the money to close the deal.

Faith is a verb.

I'll never forget seeing Tom fall to his knees, the tears spilling from his eyes, as his Father in heaven—through his father on earth—lifted the burden and replaced it with faith. My husband has never been the same. That day, faith became a verb for him too.

So, what is faith to you? Is it a noun? An inordinate, intangible thing? Or is it freedom? Is it an experience? Is it proof of God? Faith requires sacrifice. We must give over the glory, but it's an exchange; we don't have to carry the weight. James, Peter, and others tell us to consider it pure joy when we face trials in this life. Trials force us to put our faith into action.

And faith is the revelation of a relationship with a good God. 🕊

~ until next time, Wendy

Serving Our Neighbor

with **VARIOUS WRITERS**

Opportunity to serve is all around us. The following stories showcase ways in which people have chosen to be generous with their resources, whether time, money, possesions, or prayer, sometimes in the face of incredibly hard circumstances. We sincerely hope that these stories of faith encourage you to take action and stick to the paths that the Lord has prepared beforehand for you to walk in.

Words by: Elaine Starner
Originally published in May, 2015

The Drop Box

A FATHER'S HEART RESCUING LIVES

THE BELL RINGS, breaking that deep quiet of the night when everyone has been asleep for hours.

Ding dong!

Instantly the father is awake and out of his bed.

Thump, thump, thump. His heart beats just as loudly as the sound of his feet running down the stairs. What will he find this time?

On the first floor, he goes to the laundry room and opens a small door, revealing a compartment built into the wall, with an opposite door that opens to the city street outside. Inside the box in the wall is a blanket-wrapped bundle. His heart thumps more loudly.

Gently drawing out the bundle, he unfolds layers of baby blanket and finds a tiny face outlined with dark hair. He kisses the small cheeks, and cradling the baby in his arms, he bows his head and shoulders over the child, like a protecting tree, and prays, "Thank you for bringing this baby. Thank you for saving her." He asks the heavenly Father, whose heart is especially tender towards orphans, to give this little one a good home and good life.

The scene outside in the street can only be imagined. Perhaps there is a fifteen-year-old girl, lingering in the shadows, watching the door in the wall where she just placed her precious baby. She cannot see through the door. She cannot see what is happening inside the house. But still she stands, staring at the box in the wall and the words

in Korean characters above it, the words of Psalm 27:10, "Though my father and mother abandon me, the Lord will take me up."

Like the mother of Moses, who set her baby adrift to save his life, this mother is weeping and wondering what will become of her child.

· · · · · · · · ·

What else could he do? Pastor Lee Jong-rak says he had to do something; he could not live there and do nothing.

Pastor Lee, now just over sixty years old, lives in Seoul, South Korea. The capital city has ten million people living in 234 square miles. That's more people than New York City, living in less than half the area.

In this city, hundreds of babies are abandoned every year. Like Moses' mother, who was pushed to a desperate plan, most of the young mothers are also desperate. Sometimes the baby has serious health issues and the mother cannot pay for medical care. Or perhaps the mother is forced to give away the baby because she is unwed and cannot carry the shame. In Korea, a baby out of wedlock is a terrible stigma for the entire family. Or, in a society that values appearance and intellect, a young mother might feel she cannot deal with a child with Down syndrome or a physical disability.

Photos by: David Kim © Kindred Image

In 2012, the Korean government passed strict adoption laws, making it even more difficult for mothers to seek adoptive parents for their babies. And so, even more infants are abandoned as young mothers see no other choice except to leave their babies in places like parking garages or sheltered corners on the street where they hope the infants will be found and rescued.

Too often, babies die before they are found. One baby had been left in a cardboard box near the Lees' front door and almost died from the cold. Pastor Lee knew of the desperation many young women felt, even to the point of killing both themselves and their baby. He had to do something. Life is precious, and "human beings should not be thrown away like trash," he says.

So he and his wife built the baby box, he explains, "with God's heart," hoping to save as many lives as he could. A sign on the street side of the wall says, "Place to leave babies." The box gives a mother an opportunity to leave her baby at this unofficial orphanage without identifying herself or being arrested for a crime. In South Korea, it is illegal to abandon a baby (as it is in many countries).

This "drop box" for babies was installed in the Lees' wall in December of 2009. They were not sure that any babies would come, but the first baby did arrive in March of 2010. Soon the bell at the box, signaling a baby had been left, was ringing two or three times a month. After the tougher adoption laws were passed, sixteen to eighteen babies came every month. Some babies came naked, with the umbilical cord still attached. Others were accompanied by a baby bag holding clothes. By February of 2015, Pastor Lee's arms had tenderly taken up 629 babies left in the drop box.

That number is staggering. Even more terrible is the reality that most of these babies would have died if not for the shelter offered by the baby box. Pastor Lee and his wife, Chun-ja, have turned their

Pastor Lee with a crib full of his adopted children

home into a refuge and an orphanage, called the Jusarang ("God's Love") Community.

Pastor Lee and his wife could not, of course, raise all the children themselves. By law, the police must be informed when a baby is abandoned. The baby is taken to the hospital for an examination and necessary medical treatment. Most of the children will be cared for in government-run centers or foster care until and if they are adopted. Overseas adoptions are against South Korea's laws, and even adoption within the country is a long, complicated process.

Pastor Lee's heart aches to see these children shuffled from one place to another. Even though he knows he has saved a life, he says that every child also deserves a happy, loving home.

And so he and his wife have adopted children who had little chance of finding homes otherwise. Their home is a simple, three-story house in a working-class neighborhood. They have few luxuries, with none of the material abundance known by many families in the United States. What they do have in abundance is love, joy, and children. On a Christian television show in Korea, Pastor Lee recently introduced himself, with a proud smile, as the father of 19 disabled children.

"The prejudice against disabled people is severe," he says. "They are not treated as human beings. They are not respected. I am so grateful that I can help them."

Nearly all of the 19 have Down syndrome or are physically disabled. Some have severe conditions that make them unable to walk, talk, or feed themselves. One little boy has already had four heart operations. Others are busy and energetic, keeping the house in a whirlwind of activity. With a small staff, Lee and his wife give these children a mother

and a father, a home, and a happy life. One of his older boys, Ru-ri, says it is "like heaven, with people walking around like angels."

The government would not allow the Lees to officially adopt more than 9 children, but Lee says firmly that all of the children they are raising are "my children." And they are all beautiful and perfect.

"The reason I decided to become their father," Lee says, "is because God has adopted us. He has adopted me."

· · · · · · · ·

Lee Jong-rak was not always a man of compassion and love, dedicated to saving lives and giving hope.

He grew up in the country, where his parents owned a rice mill. Because he loved to play instead of work, he says, "I ended up committing many sins. I did not live a clean life."

He gained a reputation as a party-goer and ladies' man, and so he left that community and moved to Seoul. But he had trouble finding and keeping a job because he had become a heavy drinker and was often violent and destructive when drunk. Once, he was arrested for breaking windows on a bus, and a few years later at a company picnic, he punched the company president—because he was too drunk to realize what he was doing.

He met Chun-ja in Seoul. She thought he was far too skinny and called him "Fish Bones." His friends thought Chun-ja was far too short for him, and offered to find him someone taller. But the two were happy with each other and soon married.

Still, Lee could not hold a job. His drinking often ended in brawls. His wife, he says now with sadness, suffered much because of his bad habits. On Sundays, all his drinking friends came to his house and his wife was expected to cook for

> "'The prejudice against disabled people is severe,' he says. 'They are not treated as human beings. They are not respected. I am so grateful that I can help them.'"

everyone, even though there was never enough money to buy much food. One day, while drinking in a bar, Lee saw his wife walk by on the street and was stunned by how tired and hopeless she looked.

They had a daughter by now, and Lee realized he could no longer continue to live in this way. Still, he could not give up his bad habits. He applied for many jobs, but no one wanted him, and he grew more and more depressed at his failure to provide for his family.

Finally, a call came from one company. "I found out they recognized Jesus as Christ and gave glory to God." That made no difference to him. He needed the job.

On the first day he reported to work, everyone went to a morning assembly. It was a worship service. The speaker talked about Augustine, and Lee's heart was touched when he heard that this man, considered a saint, was once as depraved as he was. He grabbed the hope that one day his life could also be transformed.

Through the morning worship assemblies and the friendship of Christian co-workers, Lee came to

a place of repentance and confession of his sins. He began to attend church and changes started coming to his life. His drinking stopped. He recalls that his "heart was on fire, filled with God's peace and overwhelmed with His love. I was also constantly repentant." And he was always praying. He still is. He could not live, he says, if he could not pray.

He began praying for a son, and God granted that prayer. But it was a difficult birth and a Caesarean was necessary.

A large cyst on the side of the baby's face made his head almost twice the size of a normal infant's, and his mouth and palate were deformed. Lee, at first sight of the baby, asked God, "Why did you give me one like this?" In thirty seconds, though, he repented his thought, and instead of questioning, he thanked God for his son.

Four months later, that cyst became infected. The baby had a high fever, and on the way to the hospital, he stopped breathing and could not be revived. The doctors at the hospital told Lee and Chun-ja to give him up.

Lee prayed desperately. "God, if you were going to give him to me, why would you take him like this? Breathe your life into him." He begged for his son's life. And while he cried and prayed, the monitor above his son came to life again.

The doctors warned that the baby's brain had been deprived of oxygen too long, there would be extensive damage, and if the child lived, he would "be a vegetable." Lee would not give up. God had sent them this child. "Just save him," he told the doctors.

The doctors hesitated to remove the infected cyst, thinking the baby had little chance of surviving surgery. Lee insisted. And he prayed.

"'God, if you save him, I'll live for this child. I'll dedicate my life for the disabled children like him.' I made these vows unknowingly, out of desperation. As I was making these vows, my wife prayed too. During her prayer, she saw a vision of her husband walking up a hill like Golgotha carrying a cross. She realized it wouldn't work without the suffering of the cross. That she must carry the cross with me. At the end of our prayers, God saved his life again."

The Lees' son lived in the hospital for fourteen years. The necessary treatments seemed endless. His body, twisted and useless, had indeed lost all function, and he needed constant care. Lee, his wife, and daughter practically lived at the hospital and had to sell their home to pay medical bills.

But at the hospital, their ministry began.

Every night, Lee prayed for his son. Others with sick children soon asked him to pray for their children also. Many dying children were healed by Lee's prayers, and he led many people to know Christ.

But Lee's son was not healed. They called him Eun-man, meaning "full of God's grace."

• • • • • • • •

God changed Lee's heart as he cared for his son. In the hospital, he became known as a man of compassion and a tender heart. A woman with a granddaughter in a similar condition as Eun-man's came with a request. Would Lee also care for her granddaughter? The woman was dying, and there was no one else to take the child. The grandmother promised to believe in Jesus if Lee would care for the girl.

He felt angry and bitter that this woman would ask such a thing. But she had promised to believe in Jesus. What could he do? He agreed.

He could not tell his wife immediately. "We were in such hard and painful times. To take care of another child like our son? That's impossible." A few days before the child arrived, he told his wife, "Honey, this is what happened… I'd like to take care of this child. She has nowhere to go."

Chun-ja's response was, "If God allows it, we have to." The little girl arrived in a few days. She was completely paralyzed, and Chun-ja was the first to hold her and pray over her.

So began their ministry of protecting and cherishing life that otherwise would have been

Pictures of the Lee's happy family, with son Eun-man in the lap of Pastor Lee (pictured in the large photo)

tossed aside. Other children came in other ways. Their house filled with children of diverse ages and needs.

One wonders how they managed to support these children, many with Down syndrome or serious medical issues. Pastor Lee smiles and says now, "I am curious about that too." They balanced care of the children with a series of odd jobs. Money came in unusual ways. Others shared the burden, and God always supplied what they needed. "We always lived thankfully."

Eun-man is now almost 30 years old. He can only lie on his back and stare at the ceiling, unable to even move his head. He is fed through a tube, and two strong adults are required to bathe him because his parents cannot lift him. But life at the orphanage seems to center around his room. "The purpose for my brother's life was to build the baby box," says Ru-ri, a bright youngster who is missing fingers and toes but is president of his class and excels at taekwondo. "And the baby box saved my life."

Through Eun-man, God changed Lee's heart for a new mission. "God enabled me to love all these children."

· · · · · · · · ·

Six thousand miles away, God was preparing another heart for change. In 2011, a young man in California read the newspaper as he ate breakfast, and a story about Pastor Lee's baby box caught his eye.

His thoughts raced. The cereal was forgotten. Here was the opportunity he had dreamed of.

Brian Ivie, a 21-year-old student at the University of Southern California, had one dream—to be a famous movie producer. Since childhood, he had been making "movies" in his back yard with buddies. Now he was studying filmmaking at the university, and it was the only thing he wanted to do in life.

He saw the baby box story as his "golden ticket." A film about Lee's work could win awards and make Ivie extremely famous. After scrambling to gather the money and the crew he needed, he flew to Seoul to meet Pastor Lee and film the documentary that he hoped would win awards and make him a star in the film-making industry.

He did make the film, living in the orphanage for much of the time and sleeping on the floor with the children. A series of God-directed "coincidences" brought him to the attention of Focus on the Family, and they assisted in producing *The Drop Box*, his documentary telling the story of Pastor Lee's work. The film is now spreading the message about the value of the life of every child.

But in God's plan, Ivie did not go to Seoul only to make this film. He went because God wanted to save another child—Brian Ivie.

As Ivie's cameras documented the saving of abandoned babies, he says, "It was like a flash from heaven. Just like these kids with disabilities had crooked bodies, I have a crooked soul. And God loves me still. We're all like those kids. Bound up, in the dark, waiting for someone to come save us."

In Pastor Lee's love and care for his disabled children, Ivie saw the love of God at work in the nitty-gritty of life. "Here's a man who has given up probably every dream he ever had for himself in order to save others. That's the Gospel." Ivie learned about unconditional love that gives even when nothing can be given back. Through Eun-man, especially, he learned about the dignity and value of life bestowed by a father's love. Brian Ivie became a Christian.

He had gone to Seoul to make a movie and become famous. "I never wanted to help anyone before. But then God gave me a new heart." Now his new heart has created a non-profit organization, Kindred Image, partnering with Focus on the Family in the Global Orphan Care Fund to support Pastor Lee's work and orphan care in the United States.

"These kids are not mistakes," Ivie says. "They are important." God has sent them here for a purpose because, as Pastor Lee says, "God works for good in everything."

· · · · · · · ·

The baby box faces considerable opposition. In Korea, the government requires proper "citizen registration" at birth, and since information on parents is unavailable for these babies, none of those legalities are fulfilled. Critics say the drop box violates the children's rights, because they will never know their birth parents. Some government aid to the orphanage has been cut off. Calling the drop box illegal, the government has ordered Pastor Lee to shut it down, but he has not done so because "Saving a life is not illegal."

Children's services claim the house is too full and inadequate for so many children. A doctor should be on staff, they say, and with so many people in one house, they have tried to declare living conditions "unsanitary."

Others charge that this "mailbox for babies" encourages callous abandonment of infants. The notes that sometimes come with a baby would argue otherwise. "I am so very, very sorry. Please forgive me." "I cannot take care of my baby. I'm asking you to take him." A note might even name the child and request that the name be kept. This is not "callous" abandonment. It is heartbreaking desperation.

What will happen to this rescue operation? Pastor Lee's ultimate goal is that one day, all of human life will be cherished and there will be no need for a baby box in any country. "That's all I want." In the meantime, he is, literally, laying down his life for these children, battling serious health issues. His son, Ru-ri, class president and taekwondo expert, is already thinking of taking up his father's work one day. "That would be okay," he says firmly. "I will build on my father's work and add my own work."

Pastor Lee's dreams include new buildings that would be a place of healing for both babies and mothers. Young women forced to give up their infants are as much in need of healing love as abandoned children. Occasionally, Lee meets a mother. Given an opportunity, he shares the Gospel that can make all things new. He encourages each to be a "spiritual mother" to her child by praying for the child every day, even if she never sees her baby again. The Lees have witnessed God working in these women's lives, changing those hearts also, creating good out of terrible brokenness.

It turns out that God is the main character in this story. This story is about God's love for lost, helpless, "twisted" children—all of us, whether enslaved by addiction, abandoned on the streets of Seoul, or wandering lost in a comfortable life in the United States. It's the story of the heavenly Father who longs to adopt and love broken people and make something beautiful out of their lives.

That's how Pastor Lee would want this story to be told. 🐦

Words by: Elaine Tomski
Originally published in February, 2021

Wide Awake International

WE *ALL* ARE BELOVED

A THREE-LETTER WORD makes all the difference. Jed and Kim Johnson say YES to Jesus every day with eyes wide open and hearts wide awake. They "bring hope, dignity, and love to orphans with disabilities in Ukraine."

In 2002, Jed and Kim were married where they grew up, in the Pacific Northwest of the United States. However, they shared the hope of becoming missionaries. Kim studied nursing since she held the dream of being a nurse to orphans. "We knew orphan care was important to us and that one day we would live overseas. Somehow. We were just waiting for God to show us the place and the time." Jed and Kim were saying, "Yes!" But they sensed God saying, "Not, yet."

Get Ready

In the waiting, God was getting them ready. Kim served as a pediatric nurse in their local hospital, and Jed managed local non-profit organizations serving families and children at risk. Jed and Kim had three children: Addy, Ezra, and Havalah. And, the waiting on God's time and place for missionary service continued.

A wise Christian friend pointed out how foster kids are America's orphans. "While you're waiting, why don't you start working toward that dream?" "So," Kim says, "we became foster parents in Oregon and ended up adopting one of the foster babies in our care." In 2010, little Seth,

Jed and Kim Johnson

who had been born in drug-addiction, became a beloved family member. One evening, while Kim was up late, caring for their newest son, she stumbled upon a need she never knew existed.

"I remember the night very well. The kids were tucked into their beds for the night. Jed was working late, and I was reading a blog. By chance, or perhaps divine direction, I stumbled upon the story of a woman who had just adopted two little girls with Down syndrome from Ukraine. With each journal entry, the woman described in detail the plight of Ukrainian orphans with special needs. Several hours and a box of tissues later, I finished reading every entry." For the first time, Kim realized that people were still being treated like animals in institutions overseas. No one deserves to live in the stench of urine, tied to their beds, and isolated in silence. When Jed returned home from work, Kim sobbed, "We have to do something! We have to pray about this!"

"Are we okay with this being our future?" After lots of prayers, the answer came: Yes."

Get Set

After praying, the possibilities began to come. Kim says, "We felt really drawn to a little boy in Ukraine who needed a family. He had Apert syndrome." Apert syndrome is a genetic disorder that causes facial, skull, finger, and toe abnormalities. The bones in the face and skull fuse together too early in prenatal development, and many times a child's fingers and toes also fuse, creating a claw-like effect. Kim says, "I always thought I wasn't cut out to adopt a child with special needs." But God was using this little boy to turn their hearts toward Ukraine.

Jed and Kim realized adopting a boy with special needs meant there would be no empty nest for them. They would be caring for this little boy well into their elder years. Could they make such a commitment? They asked themselves, "Are we okay with this being our future?" After lots of prayers, the answer came: Yes.

The Johnsons started preparing all of the documents. "When you adopt from Ukraine," says Kim, "you don't get matched with a child until you are in Ukraine. So, while we were preparing the documents, another family adopted him. I was super devastated!" Kim immediately wanted to adopt another child, but Jed suggested they remain calm. Kim says, "He's always the brakes, and I'm always the gas, which makes for a good balance."

Later, while Jed was mowing the lawn, Kim says, "He was talking to the Lord like, 'God, what's this all about?' He felt God saying to him, 'Jed, I needed you to love that little boy like a father because I need you to love a lot of boys like a father.'"

So, Jed and Kim began researching how orphans with disabilities in Ukraine were being served. They discovered more than just children. Kim says, "There was a mix of all ages." They also found a quality-of-life crisis. Young men and boys created in the image of God reeked of urine, existed tied to metal bars and ignored. "No one should have to live like an animal, so what can we do about that?"

In 2012, Jed and Kim flew to Ukraine and traveled around to find answers to their questions: What's happening here? What is God doing in Ukraine? How are we supposed to respond? Kim says, "At the end of that trip, we saw that a lot of churches had programs for orphans visiting them in the institutions. But for the boys with severe disabilities, there wasn't a lot happening." Jed and Kim concluded that what they witnessed was not meeting the greater need. "When someone has been abused and neglected for so long that they can barely handle human contact, they don't need a Bible study and candy. They need out!"

Go!

At the end of that trip, Jed and Kim felt God giving them a choice. They heard Him say, "If you go back to the United States and your jobs and you raise money to support the people who are helping, I will bless you. If you come here and work to get them out, I will bless you." So, with God's blessing, the Johnsons chose yes to serving in Ukraine. They returned to the United States, started their non-profit organization, named it Wide Awake International (WAI), and established a board of directors. Then, in November of 2013, the Johnson family's time finally came to move overseas. Their dream was to get boys with physical disabilities out of institutions. Kim says, "We did not want to leave them in their suffering."

Although Jed and Kim could not speak a bit of Ukrainian, they packed twelve suitcases, five carry-ons, a guitar, and moved with their four little ones across the world.

Valuable People

In Ukraine, people with disabilities do not have value. Kim says, "There's a lot of leftover ideas from the Soviet Union, where if you can't contribute to society, then you're not of value." The Soviet Union practice of trying to hide weakness also lingers in Ukrainian culture. "The way we fulfill our mission is by showing people are made for families, not institutions. Our dream is a big goal because so many people with disabilities are tucked away in institutions."

Wide Awake International strives not only to change lives, but also change a way of thinking for an entire culture. "We work with all Ukrainians, raising up young professionals to be specialists in caring for the boys." With God's help, young Ukrainians are gaining skills to be psychologists, occupational therapists, physical therapists, and special education teachers. Because, as Kim says, "Once you take them out of the institution, that's just the beginning."

Jed and Kim began volunteering in a rural institution after moving to Ukraine. The institution for men and boys with disabilities is divided into three sections. One section houses the oldest boys and the men, a second section houses the younger boys who have aged out of the orphanage, and a third section is the isolation hall. Boys with more significant physical disabilities exist hidden away here. Sadly, many of the men and boys in Ukrainian institutions are deemed too old for adoption, so they have no chance to get out. However, first Jed and Kim searched for those boys eligible for international adoption and discovered seven teenagers. Kim is thrilled to report, "All of those boys have been adopted by Americans."

One blessed boy became a Johnson. Vladik, affectionately called Vlad, was born with Apert syndrome, just like the small boy Jed and Kim initially hoped to adopt. At the time of adoption, Vlad was a happy and social fifteen-year-old boy. When he was adopted, he was non-verbal and only made sounds. Five years later, Vlad is twenty and speaks two languages, English and Ukrainian. Kim says, "He's learned to read and write, and he is just brilliant! He's kind and so loving. Vlad doesn't really have fingers. He has thumbs, but he's a woodworker. We have a woodshop on our property where he and Jed spend hours. Vlad has his woodworking clothes and his stool, and he's curious. He calls himself Vlad the Builder. That's who he is. We would never have known that if he were still in an institution."

Jed and Kim's Ukrainian home

How many more valuable people, like Vlad, are hidden away in institutions? Too many. Yet, one by one, Wide Awake International is striving to get them out. They have gained guardianship over twenty-eight-year-old Boris, thirty-two-year-old Anton, and thirty-three-year-old Ruslan. Boris lives with the Johnsons in the remodeled old farmhouse on their rural property outside Zhytomyr, Ukraine. His diagnoses include cerebral palsy, fetal alcohol syndrome, and autism. Anton was born with a genetic disorder known as Williams Syndrome, and Ruslan lives with the affects of cerebral palsy and microcephaly. Both of these boys currently live in nearby city apartments with WAI team members.

"How many more valuable people, like Vlad, are hidden away in institutions? Too many."

Finding Ukrainians who believe in the value of all people is the key to the hope Jed and Kim have. Kim says, "We know Ukrainians are going to be the ones to solve this problem of institutions and the way their country treats people with disabilities. We don't believe we're the ones going to fix it, but that we're just supposed to be the spark."

The dream is for the next generation of Ukrainians to change their country. Wide Awake International hopes what they accomplish is replicated all across the country by Ukrainians. Kim says, "They don't need Americans to come and fix it for them. We are supposed to be an example of what can be. We don't want to provide just nice group homes with all the best therapy and equipment. We really desire something God-breathed."

"I want all of our boys to be able to find joy in something and be creative." Because their boys

have been abused and neglected for so many years, specific tasks take priority. Kim says, "First, the boys need to feel safe, get healthy, and learn how to be people because they've been raised like animals." For instance, Anton never lived with his family. Rather, he was confined to an institution from birth, for twenty-six years. "Anton's path to discovering who God made him to be is three steps forward and two steps back because he's been so broken by other people." Anton is not very verbal, but he started learning to sing about a year after living with the Johnsons. They have also discovered that Anton likes water. So, they bought him a membership to the pool. Now Anton can go with an assistant to sit and take pleasure in the calming water.

Kim says, "With our boys, as long as they're moving forward in their healing, it's a success." The process will look different for each boy. With Boris, they are just beginning to do sign language so he can learn to communicate. "He's safe and loved, and he'll blossom in his own time." Jed and Kim dream their boys are not just feeling safe but treasured. They hope the team members who live with the boys will delight in them. They desire for the boys to discover who God created them to be.

Broken

Like a culture is broken and bodies get broken, our spirits become broken, too. Jed and Kim work with adults with disabilities who have lived in an institution for twenty plus years. Kim says, "You kind of feel like nothing has prepared you to help them. Honestly, we're learning as we go along. This work requires everything, and we can't just say yes to this calling one time." Jed and Kim must say yes every single day.

"We have very broken people living with us every morning when we get up. Their healing is so long, it's going to be a forever journey," says Kim. "We've made great strides, but we're dealing with so much brokenness. Without Jesus, we cannot do it. And I try to do it on my own way too often."

Jed says, "Working with weak people shows us the brokenness in ourselves." Kim adds, "They're broken on the outside, but I'm broken on the inside because I'm selfish. And I want my time. And I want my way. And I want it on my schedule."

Jed and Kim's life demonstrates the lesson all who follow God will learn. Every day requires a new yes to Jesus and another no to self. Kim says, "I think when it gets hard, and we feel like the need is too great, we just look at the boys who are with us and see how their lives are changed."

Trusting God's Yes

Jed and Kim have learned to trust God's timing fully. "Every time we need something, it's there right when we need it. Not earlier. Just right on time." For instance, when they needed a larger van, God stepped in. While considering how to raise funds, a partner in Germany contacted them to say, "We want to give you a van!"

Wide Awake International is building a large duplex behind the Johnson's house to bring more boys out of the institution. Both sides have room for four boys. The upstairs will be living quarters for team members who will care for the boys. Kim says, "A church in England gave us money for the land." The duplex's first side was already financed before they had any team members willing to live there. It will be finished and ready by February 2021 and the second side is about sixty percent complete.

The best news came in September of 2020 when a couple from Indiana contacted Jed and Kim to say they want to be live-in assistants for the boys. Max and Morgan Martinez are committed to joining the team for at least one year. The fantastic news is that they are available to come right when the duplex is ready in February. Kim says, "God delivers right on time. That always happens to us! God meets every single need. He always shows up; this is His work. If it's important to God, He will complete it."

He has shown you, O mortal, what is good. And what does the LORD require of you? To act justly and to love mercy and to walk humbly with your God. ~ Micah 6:8

Raising American Children in Ukraine

One of the best ways to teach our children to do justice, love mercy, and walk humbly is to include them in God's purposes. Although it was a sacrifice for their children to leave the United States, they thrive in Ukraine. In November 2013, when they moved to Ukraine, the Johnsons had four children. The eight- and nine-year-olds, Ezra and Addy, were being homeschooled, which continued in their new country. Still, there were adjustments to be made. The younger two, Seth and Havalah, who were three and five, fit right into their new surroundings.

In Ukraine, people tend to be more reserved. Because of this, the Johnson family found it difficult to make friends and acquaintances. The best way to get to know people in a new community is to become involved. Kim says, "We needed to get to know people, and the kids needed to learn Ukrainian, so we put the kids in school in February. It was really hard, and they cried a lot of tears that first year. But it was the best decision we ever made! Now they're all fluent in Ukrainian and thrive here. It's their home. I'm very thankful."

Since the move from America, Kim gave birth to a sweet little girl, Evie, and they adopted Vlad in 2015. Today, the Johnsons are a full family of eight with guardianship over three additional boys. Kim says, "It's cool that since we've had the boys in our lives for seven years, this is what our kids know. Like the different behaviors, sounds, and smells the boys bring to the home. It's just our family. It's who we are, and it doesn't faze our kids."

Kim recalls how while living in the United States, their oldest daughter was frightened by

the reality of nursing home residents in wheelchairs. "Now our youngest daughter? Nothing about this life frightens her." From adults feeding adults to the noises coming from non-verbal boys, it all seems normal to her.

Kim is concerned that Ukraine doesn't offer resources to help their son, Seth. As you recall, Jed and Kim adopted Seth while he was in their foster care in the United States. His challenges originate with a drug-addicted birth mother. "I sometimes worry about his future," says Kim. "Then, I see he has the softest heart for Boris." Boris is a non-verbal, clumsy walking, twenty-eight-year-old the size of a nine-year-old. "And our Seth, who has his own struggles, is so gentle and kind with Boris. I think he needed the boys." Concerning all of her children, Kim says, "For whatever God is growing them up to be, they needed this."

The Johnson family cannot do as many things as other families. They move slower and currently they need to protect their boys from the threat of the Covid-19 virus. Kim says, "If they get sick in Ukraine, it's not going to go well. They don't get good care in the hospital, so we have to find the balance of living our own lives and protecting our boys. We have to adjust for the people in our family who are weaker."

"Our journey to Ukraine and our journey in Ukraine is a journey of simply saying yes. There is no greater value in one person's yes over another," says Kim. All Christ-followers who keep their eyes wide open and ears wide awake will receive the Holy Spirit's guidance. He has been leading the Johnson family ever since Jed and Kim took their marriage vows. The Johnsons claim, "We're just two people who fell in love with Jesus and decided to say yes to the next thing He presented to us." As a result, some of the world's most marginalized people are now beloved. 🕊

Words by: Nic Stoltzfus
Originally published in June, 2022

Prayers for the Taken

THE STORY OF THE HAITI HOSTAGE CRISIS

"But I say to you, love your enemies, bless those who curse you, do good to those who hate you, and pray for those who spitefully use you and persecute you." ~ Matthew 5:44

IN PORT-AU-PRINCE, HAITI, around a hundred gangs fight for control of the capital city. After the president of Haiti was assassinated in July 2021, the gang fighting worsened, and the entire nation plunged into chaos. Gangs frequently use kidnapping as a way to finance their work. In 2020, nearly 800 people were kidnapped, and in 2021, the number was even higher. In April 2021, the 400 Mawozo gang captured a Catholic priest and nun from France, along with eight others from their commune. The ransom the gang demanded for their release was $1 million. It is unclear whether the ransom was paid, but two weeks after the initial kidnapping, the 400 Mawozo gang had released all the hostages.

Seven months after their April kidnapping—and three months after the president's assassination—this same gang kidnapped another group of missionaries: seventeen people serving in Haiti with Christian Aid Ministries.

The Kidnapping

It was a Saturday in mid-October, and the morning was sunny, with the temperature a balmy and tropical 70 degrees. In the village of Titanyen, located northwest of Port-au-Prince, seventeen missionaries had their heads bowed in prayer.

Those gathered in prayer were six men, six women, and five children. The adults ranged in age from 18 to 48, and the children were ages eight months, 3, 6, 13, and 15. One man was from Ontario, Canada, and the rest were from various American states—Michigan, Ohio, Oregon, Pennsylvania, Tennessee, and Wisconsin. They were all missionaries with Christian Aid Ministries (CAM).

CAM has worked in Haiti for over 30 years, and the work they do includes ministering to orphans and widows; supplying medical clinics throughout the country; delivering nutritional products to malnourished children; rebuilding homes destroyed by earthquakes; offering biblical-based leadership training to teachers and pastors; and paying wages to Haitian workers improving their communities through repairing roads, clearing canals, and laying water lines.

The missionaries were gathered outside, and they prayed for safety and protection. They planned to drive to an orphanage in the small village of Ganthier, located around 25 miles away, and they would be heading through areas known for gang activity. Haiti is one of the poorest countries in the world—one out of every two Haitians lives below the poverty line, three out of every four don't have clean water, and one out of every

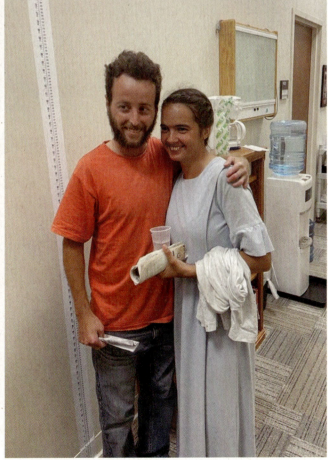

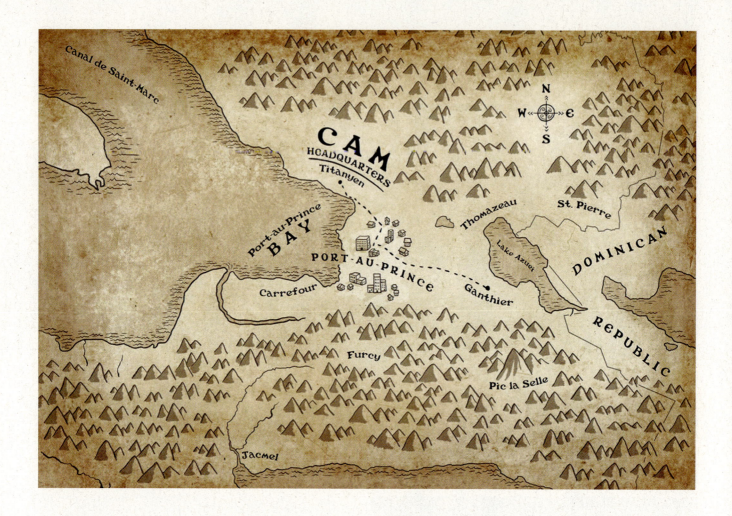

four can't read. These missionaries serving with Christian Aid Ministries in Haiti were there with one goal in mind: to share Jesus' transformative love with the Haitian people.

· · · · · · · · ·

The drive to the orphanage was mostly uneventful, and the missionaries arrived about an hour after they left CAM's base in Titanyen. The missionaries spent three hours with the children at the orphanage, playing soccer and other games, and left around one o'clock after a time of fellowship and a fried chicken dinner. The trouble began on the way home. A few miles west of the orphanage, the road was blocked by an ambulance and a truck laid crossways across the road. Knowing that this stretch of road is known for gang activity, the driver did not want to stop, so he yanked the steering wheel to the side, making a tight U-turn,

and headed back in the direction of the orphanage. In the rearview mirror, the driver saw a small white Ford pickup with gunmen in the back racing towards them. These armed men demanded that they follow them, so the driver turned back toward the roadblock. The pickup diverted the van off the main road and down a bumpy trail. The armed men stopped the van again, yanked the driver out of the van, roughed him up, and forced him into one of the other vehicles. The other missionaries were afraid they'd never see him again. One of the armed men got into the driver's seat, slammed his foot on the accelerator, and sped recklessly over the pothole-riddled road, trying to keep up with the pickup truck. During this time, one of the missionaries shared his location in a text thread with over two hundred people. Another one texted CAM's Haiti Country Director: "Please pray, the gang has taken us. We're being kidnapped."

The dirt road dead-ended in a circular clearing, and the missionaries in the van saw a shack to their left and a house to their right. The ambulance that had blocked the road and another SUV pulled into the clearing, and gang members with assault rifles poured out of the vehicles. The gang members ordered the missionaries out of the van and took everyone's phones and cash. The gang members brought out the driver and stood all seventeen missionaries in a line against the wall of the house that the gang members called "The Devil's House." The hostages feared that they were going to be executed by the gang. Despite their trepidation, they prayed and repeatedly sang the song *The Angel of the Lord*, based on Psalm 34, verses 7 and 8:

"The angel of the Lord encampeth round about them that fear him, and delivereth them. O taste and see that the Lord is good. Blessed is the man that trusteth in Him."

The gang members yelled at them to stop singing, but the missionaries continued anyway. After taking everyone's shoes, the gang ordered the missionaries towards the shack. This concrete shack had a porch and two rooms; both rooms were already filled with hostages, so the gang members removed two Haitian hostages from one of the rooms to make room for the missionaries. The seventeen walked barefoot into the now-empty room: it was windowless and small—roughly ten feet wide by twelve feet long—and they crammed next to one another to fit inside. After they got in, the guards boarded the door shut. Mosquitoes whined around their heads, slipping in through cracks in the door, and fire ants crawled over their bare feet. It was a sweltering 90 degrees outside, and it felt just as hot crammed inside the small room. As their eyes adjusted to the darkened room, the missionaries noticed the concrete walls were pockmarked with bullet holes and splattered with blood. The children cried, everyone's hearts pounded against their chests, and adrenaline-triggered sweat dripped down their bodies. Amid this stress and fear, the missionaries sought peace through prayer and song. In a testimony given to his home church in Wisconsin, one missionary said, "The acoustics were pretty good [in that room], so we sat there and sang. It was encouraging to sing together."

That evening the leader of the gang had one of the missionaries call CAM's Haiti Country Director. After he confirmed to the Country Director that they were all safe, the leader grabbed the phone from the missionary and spoke to the Country Director directly.

The gang leader said, "Everybody is in my hand, and I'm in control. I have them all. They're all in my hand... I need one million dollars for each, or I kill them all."

The Country Director was shocked by this number: seventeen million dollars to free everyone. CAM has a no-ransom policy, and he knew that they would not pay the ransom. So, the Country Director calmly replied, "We're missionaries. We're here working for God. We're not going to give you money. You got the wrong people—these people are children of God."

The gang leader screamed back, "You don't talk. You're not in a position to talk. I do the talking—the money or they die!" And then he hung up the phone.

Immediately the US government got involved with the hostage situation, and they began working with the Haitian authorities and CAM on a plan to free the hostages. They realized that

> **"They knew the dangers involved with serving in Haiti, but they chose to leave the comfort of their homes to help the Haitian people."**

the missionaries had been captured by the 400 Mawozo gang, the same gang that had kidnapped ten Catholic missionaries earlier that year. The news spread around the world, and phone calls and e-mails poured into Christian Aid Ministry's headquarters in Holmes County, Ohio. The staff there began holding twice-daily conference calls via phone with the family members, and they brought in Christian counselors with experience in traumatic situations.

Meanwhile, back in Haiti, the 400 Mawozo gang pressed harder for the ransom money. Five days after he kidnapped the seventeen missionaries, the gang leader released a video on social media where he said, "I swear by thunder if I don't get what I'm asking for, I will put a bullet in the heads of these Americans."

The same day that the gang leader released his life-threatening message, the family members of the hostages released this life-affirming message:

Dear Church of Christ around the world, Thank you for your prayers on behalf of our family members who are being held hostage in Haiti. God has given our loved ones the unique opportunity to live out our Lord's command to, "love your enemies, bless them that curse you, do good to them that hate you" (Matthew 5:44). God invites us to call upon His name in the day of trouble. (Psalm 50:15) We thank Him that He is God and ask Him to hear our prayers and bring our families home. We also pray that the light of God's love might shine out into the darkness of sin, and that the gang members might be freed from their bondage to sin and experience freedom in Jesus Christ. Thank you, brothers and sisters in Christ, and PLEASE keep praying!

Day to Day Life

The missionaries struggled with unclean water, insect bites, infections, boredom, spiritual distress, terror, and disagreements on whether to escape or

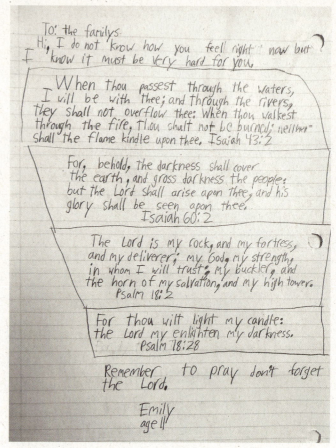
A letter written to the families of the kidnapped missionaries

remain captive. Yet, amidst these tribulations, they created a daily rhythm centered around living out their faith. They began their days with prayers and singing, which would sometimes last until noon. At one pm every day, they prayed for deliverance. And in the evening, they ended the day with singing and prayers.

The one missionary who spoke the most Creole preached the Gospel every night to the guards, they all invited the guards to have church with them on Sundays, shared Bible verses with one another from memory, and—through it all—the group continued to sing. According to one missionary, the songs they sang the most included *There is a God [Beyond the Azure Blue], One More Miracle, Come Bless the Lord, We've Got the Power,* and *Unto Thee O Lord.*

The gang did look after the missionaries. They allowed them time outside, provided fresh coconuts and mango for them, brought fans so they could cool off, and ensured that they had access to hygiene products. They did not physically abuse the missionaries and paid particular attention to the children's health. But all of this was done in a cold and calculating way. In their eyes, taking care of the missionaries was no different than taking care of a business asset—they wanted a good return on investment, so why would they risk someone dying and losing a million dollars?

One of the missionaries shared about the behavior of the gang members:

"Those men made no bones about it that they serve Satan... there was a lot of smoking and lots of drugs. [One of the gang members] would sell cigarettes and cocaine to the guards. Whenever the battery on the radio would stand for it, the guards would listen to terrible music... women would come around that were obviously up to no good. There was also a lot of cursing. The battle between light and darkness was very obvious at that place."

• • • • • • • •

After ten days at the first location, the gang moved the seventeen missionaries to a new location, spooked by news they heard over their radio of the US military coming to Haiti. After three-and-a-half weeks at the new location, the gang moved them back to their first location: the small concrete shack. Not long after bringing the missionaries back to the shack, they released two of them—a husband and wife. The gang released them because they didn't have the medical supplies they needed to care for the husband. In addition, they may have feared reprisal from the US government if he died as a hostage.

Four days after two of the missionaries were freed, the remaining fifteen celebrated Thanksgiving. The guards gave them Haitian stew, and the change of meal from the regular rice and beans was appreciated, but their homesickness was particularly sharp this day. Back in the US and Canada, families of the hostages also yearned to have their loved ones back home at the supper table. It had been over a month since their loved ones had been kidnapped. They struggled with feeling helpless, yet they continued to pray. One family member shared, "...although I really can't do anything from here for our loved ones, I can pray, and God can take my petition, and thousands more like mine and do BIG things... Hallelujah!"

During this time, those working for the release of the hostages told CAM that an anonymous party had offered to pay the ransom. CAM was under pressure to put money on the table to negotiate with the gang for the release of the hostages. As CAM management—in light of a no-ransom policy—agonized over the decision of whether or not to pay the ransom, this offer came. With prayerful consideration, CAM agreed to hand negotiations over to others, agreeing that ransom funds from the anonymous donor would be offered.

On the first Sunday of December, the gang released three more missionaries. This was a bittersweet moment for one of the missionaries who had been released: she was reunited with her husband, but four of her children were still being held hostage.

Even though a ransom was paid before these three missionaries were released, the gang didn't let the remaining twelve hostages go. The hostages were not aware of any of this—they were busy planning their escape.

The Escape

During Sunday services and meeting times, the group discussed escape and deliverance. In a journal that he kept during this time (written with a pen on pieces of paper towel), one of the missionaries wrote the following concerning the subject:

We had church this morning, but with food, liberty, and stories as our topics. Stories of people being delivered and how God delivered us. Another topic we discussed was faith. How do faith and works work together? How do our wants and wishes mesh with what God wants for us? We discussed that topic a lot. Is faith just believing God can do something, and then we sit back and wait? Or is it believing that God will do something and then we react because we believe God is going to have our backs? Do we step out? Are we the ones to make the first move? A lot of that discussion had discussions of escape along with it. We gave God a lot of good ideas on how to deliver us.

Of the twelve who remained—a married couple, four single men, two single women, and four children—the decision on whether to attempt an escape weighed heavily on them. They prayed constantly for discernment.

The remaining twelve hostages finally came to an agreement, and they decided to escape in the middle of the night. The sunset on the eve of their escape attempt was stunning, and a rich array of colors transformed the sky into a fiery blaze. As the missionaries watched the sunlight fade into twilight, they prayed and sang *Is that the Lights of Home?*

The group had planned to escape at one that morning, but it took nearly two hours until the guards settled down. According to one hostage, "The guards were super worked up. They were smoking and jamming out on their radios and drinking and getting up at random times and walking around, and it just didn't look like they were ever going to settle down and give us an actual good 10-15 minutes to make an attempt at the back door."

Finally, around 3 am, the group opened the door into the moonlit yard. The guards were distracted, playing with their phones and not paying attention to the shack. The generator rumbling nearby covered the sounds of their footfalls as they stepped over briars and brambles and crept to the edge of the brush. With bags of water in their pockets, one of the women carrying the baby, and one of the men shouldering the toddler, the ten missionaries on foot walked for miles, moving as fast as they could away from the gang. They walked through the underbrush, past barking dogs, across a sleepy village, and between cacti with sharpened barbs that stung their feet and ankles. Finally, they heard cars from a distant highway and soon reached a village nearby.

Not long after daybreak, the two missionaries who spoke the most Creole found a Haitian man willing to help them. He let them use his phone, and they called CAM's Haitian Country Director. The missionary told the Country Director that they had all escaped, and he said, "The Lord delivered us."

After two months of captivity, they were finally free.

· · · · · · · ·

After the missionaries arrived back safe in Canada and the US, they continued to pray for the people of Haiti, even the members of the 400 Mawozo gang who had kidnapped them and held them hostage. In their press release, Christian Aid Ministries included a specific message to the kidnappers:

We do not know all of the challenges you face. We do believe that violence and oppression of others can never be justified. You caused our hostages and their families a lot of suffering. However, Jesus taught us by word and by His own example that the power of forgiving love is stronger than the hate of violent force. Therefore, we extend forgiveness to you. The hostages told you plainly how you can also be forgiven by God, if you repent. Our desire is that you and all who hear or read this statement may come to the saving knowledge of Jesus Christ, our Savior, the Son of God, and the Prince of Peace. Jesus died for all so that all can be saved. 🐦

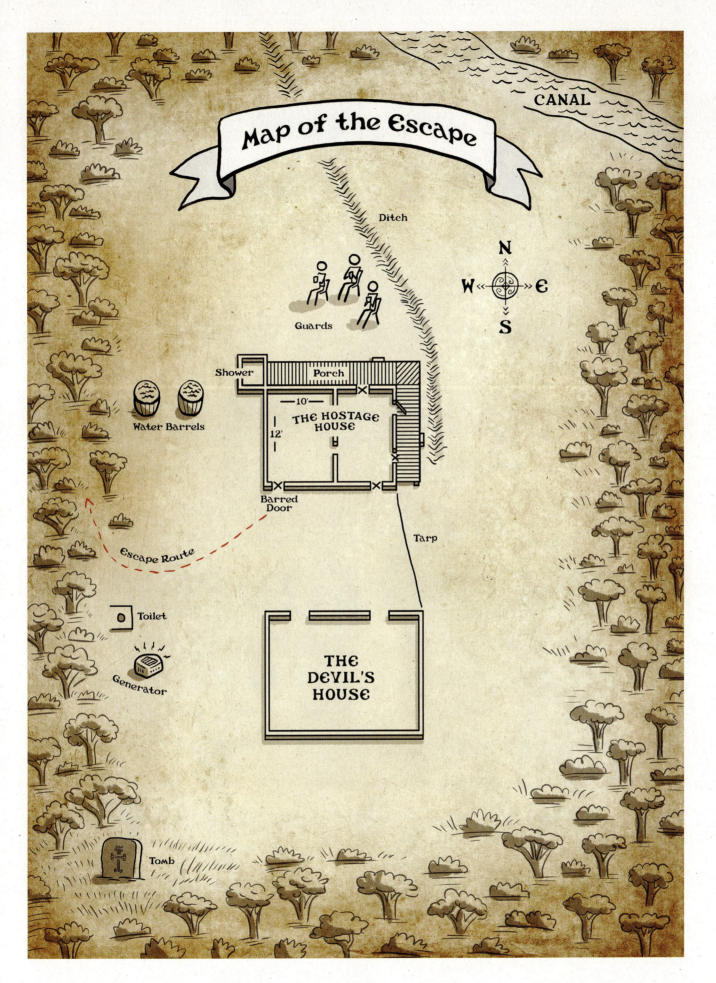

Words by: Sabrina Schlabach
Originally published in August, 2022

The First Year

ANDREW & CASSEY GOLDEN'S ADOPTION STORY

AS THEY STOOD in their bathroom, Andrew and Cassey Golden were surprised to learn that they were pregnant with their third child. However, there would be a nine-year gap between the baby and the next oldest. Andrew and Cassey wanted their newest addition to have a sibling close to his own age. For Cassey, this cemented the idea that they were meant to adopt. "Adoption was something that had been on our minds when we first started our family, but as Ava and Aiden grew older, and life got busier, that thought became fleeting," said Andrew.

Andrew and Cassey originally decided upon international adoption. They began the home study process for adopting a child from Colombia through the special needs program. "While special needs may not have originally been on our minds, God took us on a journey to seeking it out," shared Cassey. One day they had a conversation with a friend who had adopted domestically through NDSAN (National Down syndrome Adoption Network). The Goldens decided to move their home study from international to domestic adoption, also through NDSAN. They were approved for two children, which meant they could adopt siblings or twins.

In July 2021, the Golden's profile was shown to a family looking for parents to adopt twin boys. Not just any twin boys: identical twin boys both with Down syndrome, a very rare occurrence. They knew the timing was crazy to adopt two children. Andrew was in the middle of a fellowship at school, and Cassey was caring for their three children, the youngest of which she was still nursing. However, they didn't want to pass up an opportunity God gave them just because of timing. So Andrew and Cassey said yes.

On July 13, the Goldens were scheduled to have a phone conversation with the biological family to help narrow down their choices. But the unexpected happened. After receiving a phone call stating that the mother was in the hospital due to complications, the phone call was moved to the next day, July 14. Cassey and the children were visiting family, but they still had the phone call, with Andrew joining in from home in Texas. A few hours later, the Goldens received word that they were chosen to adopt the boys. Cassey was preparing to drive down to Alabama the next day to be present for the birth of the twins. Seven minutes later, another call came stating that one of the boys' heart rate had dropped and the babies would be born immediately. Cassey shared, "We hadn't even told the children that we were chosen. I quickly explained the situation to the kids: we were chosen to adopt. Oh, and there's not one baby, there's two, and they are being born right away. I'm leaving immediately for Alabama."

Cassey arrived in Birmingham to meet the biological parents and the newborn boys. Jude and Asher were born on July 14 at thirty weeks and five days, weighing in at 2 pounds 4 ounces and 2 pounds 5 ounces. Because of their prematurity and Down syndrome, they faced several hurdles. Jude and Asher were born with BPD (Bronchial Pulmonary Dysplasia), both had small holes in their hearts, and Jude possibly has PVL (meaning he has some brain damage from birth, and as of now, they're unsure the extent of the damage. It typically means some delays in learning and development). The boys would be in the NICU (Neonatal Intensive Care Unit) for a while, which complicated things for the adoption.

The following two-and-a-half months were difficult for the Golden family. Cassey lived at the Ronald McDonald house one block away from the hospital and spent most of her time with Jude and Asher. Andrew flew in every other weekend; when he wasn't there, he was in school, working, and trying to keep the house going. Andrew said, "We had family and friends that were taking shifts, staying with the kids to help keep everything going. It was a uniquely humbling situation to see how God brought all the pieces together." Cassey added, "We're both type A personalities and like to have things organized and in control. This was very outside of our comfort zone."

Cassey commented that Andrew was good at making her get out of the hospital and take a walk, get fresh air, and eat something other than hospital food. One weekend the whole family converged in Birmingham. While Andrew spent time with Jude and Asher, the children spent some time with their mom. Cassey did go home a couple of times, most importantly on Ava and Aiden's first day of school. "This was a big deal because up until this point, I had homeschooled. We had just recently made the difficult decision to attend public school."

As Jude and Asher were in the NICU, Cassey worked alongside the nurses to get the twins used to bottle-feeding. "It was such an isolating situation. I became very close with the nurses, the staff at the Ronald McDonald house, and the lactation consultant. I'm so grateful for their comfort and support," said Cassey. "Many people that have a baby in NICU are trying to wrap their heads around the medical diagnosis, what their lives will look like now. That wasn't the case for us. We pursued this. So that side of things wasn't difficult; it was the separation from family and everything normal."

> "Jude and Asher were born on July 14 at thirty weeks and five days, weighing in at 2 pounds 4 ounces and 2 pounds 5 ounces."

After Jude and Asher graduated from NICU, Cassey still needed to remain in Alabama because of adoption paperwork. Thankfully, one of those wonderful nurse's mother offered a place for them to stay. Cassey's mom came down to help as well. "The boys were on and off oxygen, and now every feeding and diaper change was all on us. It was a learning experience," Cassey said, "but in the end, it was good to have that little bit of time to get used to it before heading home and jumping into caring for five kids." It was three months in all before Cassey brought the boys home to Texas. "I was worried especially how Kai would handle it since he was only 18 months old and much of my attention would be diverted in caring for two very needy babies." She needn't have worried. Kai is absolutely enamored with Jude and Asher. Often, when Cassey wakes Kai from his nap, he will hear the boys and immediately say, "Babies. Babies," looking for them. "It is so fun to watch that bond develop, knowing that they are close in age and will go through life together," shared Cassey.

"It has been an exceptionally hard year, but we can see the light at the end of the tunnel. Andrew will graduate from his fellowship, and a week later, Jude and Asher turn one," said Cassey. "It doesn't mean that everything will suddenly be easier, but it feels like such a milestone, like we're through the hardest part of it." The twins are doing very well. They are no longer on oxygen, and the holes in their hearts have closed. Jude and Asher are gaining weight (although it is still sometimes a struggle to get them to take in enough calories), and therapists come out twice a week for physical, occupational, and speech therapies.

While this year has been full of upheaval, the Goldens see and appreciate the glimmers of hope they've received throughout. "God has kept me grounded, and I've recentered on family and family values," Andrew shared. The friends, family, and church around them have been such a blessing. "That first weekend when we were in the hospital, there was so much mystery about what was happening. Then we received a phone call from Marlin Miller. While we had never heard of him or Room to Bloom, they were sending us a check to help cover the cost of the adoption," said Andrew. Cassey added, "Do you know the hope and reassurance we felt when we got that call? Here is this unexpected money we didn't have to apply for, no strings attached! There are grants available, but the paperwork is daunting, especially when we were already filling out tons of paperwork for the adoption. It had been such a hard day; then we received that call. I just cried."

Reflecting on Room to Bloom's gift, Andrew said, "That made us a part of another vibrant and robust community... we are grateful for the people that support Room to Bloom and actively make choices to support orphans through adoption, being the hands and feet of Christ." 🐔

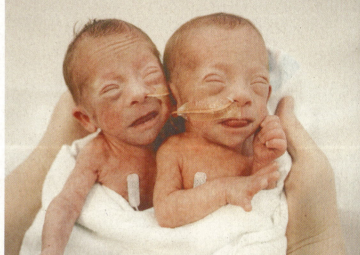

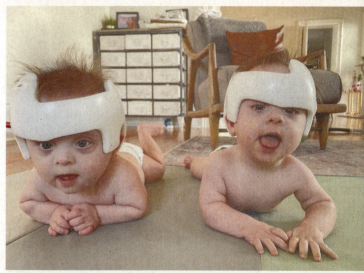

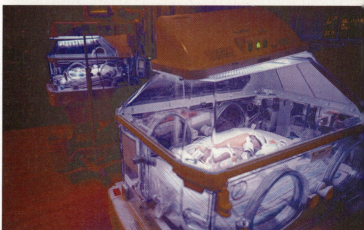

Words by: Sabrina Schlabach
Originally published in March, 2023

Remarkable Joy

THE WURDEMAN ADOPTION STORY

I'M SURE EACH OF US has met someone, whether it's a stranger or a treasured friend, whose smile radiates with joy. It's a contagious smile, full of light and devoid of any judgement. We can't help but smile in return. In that moment, the lighthearted feeling of pure delight brings an unmistakable peace amid all the other thoughts clamoring for our attention. Those are the kinds of moments, and people, that we are drawn to and cherish.

For Brice and Amanda Wurdeman, they experienced that remarkable joy when their youngest son Rusk was born. While all of their children are special and bring joy to the family, Rusk has the distinction of being born with Down syndrome. "We didn't really know anything about caring for a child with special needs, but what people say is true—they really do bring an extra joy," shared Amanda. This also spurred something in Brice's heart, and he was ready to adopt.

· · · · · · · ·

Children have always been a part of Brice and Amanda's life. They spent 15 years in the mission field growing hearts for Jesus and growing their family. In Haiti they lived near orphanages, in St. Vincent they assisted with a preschool, and they have often cared for the children beyond their four walls. All throughout her life, from a very young age, Amanda was interested in adoption, however Brice did not

feel that same call. So, Amanda remained content in ministering to her children and all the kids she encountered.

In April 2020, Rusk was born with Down syndrome. Together the family began learning how to care for a child with special needs, and as they did so, they discovered just how precious and full of joy Rusk is. Even though the Wurdemans had worked with children and orphanages, Amanda shared, "I'm so sad to say that we avoided and ignored those kids that had special needs, just like everyone else. We didn't know how to 'handle those kids.' Once Rusk was born, he really changed our hearts."

For Amanda, having six children and not getting any younger, it had settled in her heart that they were done having kids; it was time to close that chapter. However, Brice's heart began stirring and he told Amanda, "We should adopt." After the initial surprise of finally hearing those words, she was all in. Amanda shared that they didn't choose to adopt so that Rusk could have a "buddy," it was because they saw the need out there and knew the joy that children with Down syndrome bring. "There's other kids that need a family and we know how to do this," she said.

Throughout their missionary service, the Wurdemans had learned to pray: *God, whatever Your will is for us, we want to be there.* "But this time we prayed very specifically. We asked God that if there's a little boy with Down syndrome for us, to

please show us," said Amanda. For several months, they were actively reaching out to NDSAN (National Down syndrome Adoption Network) and the countries they served in, seeking that child.

This was not an easy road, and quite frustrating—to the point that they thought perhaps this is not what God had for them. Foster care told them they had too many kids and weren't a good fit. NDSAN said the chances of being picked were slim because of their age and six kids. Haiti had such a long wait that they hesitated to go that route; and the woman from the orphanage in St. Vincent told them it was never going to happen. Had they misheard God? Was their desire to adopt never going to be realized?

In May 2021, having just moved back to the U.S., the woman from St. Vincent reached out to Amanda. She wrote a letter saying that she had the perfect little boy for them; he had Down syndrome and was only one week younger than Rusk! This was exciting news, and they began picturing their little Caribbean boy. What Brice and Amanda didn't know was that this woman worked with orphanages from several countries, and their little boy was actually from Serbia.

The Wurdemans, after seeing a picture of a cute, healthy, round-cheeked boy—and praying— quickly said yes to Sutter. The adoption process in Serbia is a little different than in the States: First a child is matched, and then the home study process begins. Now that Brice and Amanda said yes, they had to submit a letter to the Serbian government about their family and their desire to adopt Sutter. Serbia said yes and the long paperwork task began.

"We initially received two videos, five pictures, and some doctor's notes," stated Amanda. "Then we got nothing—for 13 months." It was a difficult waiting period, but they were committed to Sutter. It helped that Amanda was able to connect with a group of women who had also adopted from Serbia. "It's a very small group since Serbia only allows 4-6 adoptions per year [to outside countries]," she said, "but they were able to give tips and advice on how everything worked." They learned that only one family can travel at a time, it would be a three-week trip requiring both Brice and Amanda, and that Serbia shuts down during the summer. Which meant it was unlikely that they would be allowed immediate entry—even after months of waiting.

Our God, however, is not limited by worldly restrictions. He opened the doors for the Wurdemans to travel to Serbia in July. Amanda was excited to meet Sutter and talk to the orphanage, to find out how they cared for him. What she found was not at all what was expected. After Sutter had been matched with them, he moved from the baby floor to the older children's floor. In that time, he basically reverted to an unhealthy newborn. Sutter was unable to hold up his head, he laid in his crib all day, and only got a few syringes of pureed food. Sutter only weighed 17 pounds at the age of 2. (Amanda was just glad they got him when they did, as there were much older children laying nearby that weighed about the same as Sutter.)

As the Wurdemans prepared for the adoption finalization, the orphanage disclosed that Sutter had epilepsy. This resulted in him receiving medication which heavily sedated him. "He could barely wake

up when we were there," Amanda said. "They told me that it was normal, but we thought, 'no, this is not how a two-year-old should be.' Something was wrong." The Wurdemans knew that they wouldn't be walking into a perfect situation with over 200 children in the orphanage, but it was worse than they had expected.

Brice and Amanda visited Sutter at the orphanage for one week, then they spent two weeks getting to know each other while waiting on paperwork and going to doctor's appointments. The plane ride home brought its own challenges. "Sutter didn't like to be touched. He wasn't used to it," shared Amanda. "So, we laid him on the seat between us to try and keep him calm, all while others were shouting at us in Serbian to pick up our kid." And changing his diaper has been a trial, too. He just screams, making Amanda fear what had been done to him. "The mom's group told me that was normal. At the orphanage they strip off the diaper and spray them down with cold water," she said. Naturally, that is a traumatic experience.

In the few months since they've been home, they took Sutter to several different doctors and specialists to find out exactly what he needs. They've been adjusting his medication, and since July, he's begun to improve. The doctors told them to treat him like a newborn. Take it one step at a time and surround him with love. Sutter can now hold his head up, is beginning to eat more food, goes to speech, occupational, and physical therapy (along with Rusk), and enjoys interacting with his family.

The Wurdemans pray that more people's hearts would be opened to adoption. Amanda shared that they felt called to adopt and trusted that God would provide—so much so, that they didn't really look into the cost of adoption. They were astounded that it was nearly $42,000. "But there are so many grants available, and God absolutely did provide. Don't let the cost of adoption scare you off. If God calls you to it, He'll provide for it." Every twinkly-eyed smile that warms our hearts with joy far outweighs the cost. 🐦

Words by: Sabrina Schlabach
Originally published in January, 2024

Bold Prayers

JOE AND DEVON HUDGENS' ADOPTION STORY

ONE EVENT CAN SHIFT THE COURSE of our lives. Good or bad. Ready or not. For Joe and Devon Hudgens, that moment came when someone close to them, who was pregnant, realized the baby would have Down syndrome. Despite Devon's attempts to reach out and counsel, constant prayers, and offer of adoption, the mother decided to abort the baby. Devon struggled through a very traumatic and difficult time because of that devastating decision. But, as the saying goes, hindsight is 20/20, and she can now see that God knew what was going to happen; how He used that experience to plant a seed in her heart. A seed of adoption.

While this seed was being planted, the Hudgenses were reading a book with their church called *Dangerous Prayers* by Craig Groeschel. The book was challenging them to step outside of their comfort zone. "Our life is not our own. If I can die to self and ask God to search my heart, break my heart, and say send me... That's a scary prayer," said Devon. "But that's what we prayed. If God is calling you to something, He will provide. He's proven that over and over."

This mindset got them thinking. "If we were willing to adopt that one baby, why can't we do this for someone else?" shared Devon. Joe added, "We felt like things were stacked against us. We're old–well, not that old, but we're not 25, and we can't afford it. But what did Jesus really mean when He said, 'I came to give you life and give it more abundantly'? It's not comfort that can be found in the things of the world because that will let us down. The abundant life is the life lived for Christ." So, they began praying, trusting God with taking the next step, and He was opening doors.

The Hudgenses were accepted by Nightlight Christian Adoptions on October 21, 2020—one day before their future son was born! It took a while to go through the paperwork and home study process, but eventually, they connected with NDSAN (National Down Syndrome Adoption Network) and moved further along the adoption path. Every time Joe and Devon felt unsure, God would send another sign that they were on the right path. And, in May of 2021, their profile was ready to be shown to potential families.

"Our original plan was to adopt a baby. That's where our hearts were, but we determined that we would say yes to every child, no matter the medical diagnosis," Devon said. "God would handle the details." In the mounting anticipation, Devon sent an email to NDSAN asking how often they see "not-so-young" couples get chosen. The response? Few and far between. "My heart seized for a moment. I shouldn't have sent the email—only because the answer discouraged me," shared Devon. "But then I reminded myself that it's okay. God led us to this." God was indeed handling the details. Within one week, they had their first presentation of a baby.

Within a month, they were presented with five babies and said yes to all of them.

In June, Joe and Devon were matched with Jack, an 8-month-old boy with Down syndrome. And in July they were scheduled to meet the birth father. About two weeks before they were scheduled to meet, the Hudgenses were on their annual camping trip when Devon began having terrible pain in her neck and jaw. While having pain at times wasn't new to Devon–who has a diagnosis of non-terminal multiple sclerosis–this was a new one. And it didn't just go away. It was causing numbness that affected her speech and her mouth began to droop. As the meeting loomed ahead, Devon cried out to God, asking and trusting Him to get her through this meeting and that the father would see whatever he needed to see. Again, God came through in a miraculous way. Not only did the meeting go well, but an hour afterward they received the call that the father wanted to continue moving forward with the adoption. "God is so good," said Devon.

Less than a month later, in August, Joe and Devon welcomed Jack into their family. Although he was 10 months old, Jack behaved like a newborn and had some very serious health issues. His head would jerk back and forth, so the Hudgenses braced his head to protect him. "Most of the time Jack just laid there," said Devon. "He didn't respond to lights or our faces. It was so scary, and I feared that he was blind too." Thankfully, Jack wasn't blind, but he was diagnosed with Infantile Spasms. The spasms were caused by a combination of slow brain waves and high electrical activity.

Because Jack was so young, they had to inject his ACTH Steroid medication. "It was awful," said Devon. "The needles were huge and looked like they'd go right through his bones." The shots were given twice a day and caused swelling and heightened blood pressure. A second round of treatment was prescribed, but they only made it about halfway through before they had to stop. Devon said, "Jack's blood pressure went alarmingly high.

It was a hard, hard time." Thankfully though, the recent EEG tests have shown much improvement, and he's stopped having spasms.

As of April 2023, Jack is a little over two years old. Even though he's still only at the level of a 10-month-old, he's doing really well. Jack is a happy little guy that loves to smile and laugh. He can scoot toward Joe and Devon, and he can sit up. Jack loves his splash pad, his rattle, and music. "When Jack is upset, I'll start singing to him, and he immediately calms down," shared Devon. He also loves to eat–and he's not picky! He will eat whatever the rest of the family is eating.

A crucial part of success is community. The Hudgenses feel so blessed by the people around them and their church family. They literally had forty people show up to Jack's adoption hearing. "Community has absolutely made this possible. You can't do it alone," said Devon. "Knowing that people think of you, care for you, and pray for you is vital."

One of the lessons the Hudgenses have learned is to not be afraid to pray those *dangerous prayers* and step out in faith once they feel the Lord's calling. It's like stepping off a cliff–not in a bad way–into a new adventure, knowing that God is directing every step of the journey. "Looking back," said Devon, "we were happy with our family of three. Our other son is a teenager, and we were ready to move into the next phase of life. We didn't know we were missing Jack. Now there's four of us and we couldn't imagine life without him." 🐦

"Jack's adoption hearing was on June 24, 2022—the same day that Roe v. Wade was overturned. The significance isn't lost on us. It's amazing to think that abortion is what led us on the journey to Jack."